JAYDN DEWALD
Sheets of Sound:
Notes on Music & Writing

BROKEN SLEEP BOOKS

All rights reserved; no part of this book
may be reproduced by any means
without the publisher's permission.

Published 2020,
Broken Sleep Books:
Cornwall / Wales

brokensleepbooks.com

The author has asserted their right to be
identified as the author of this Work in
accordance with the Copyright, Designs
and Patents Act 1988

First Edition

Lay out your unrest.

Publisher/Editor: Aaron Kent

Typeset in UK by Aaron Kent

Broken Sleep Books is committed to
a sustainable future for our planet,
and therefore uses print on
demand publication.

brokensleepbooks@gmail.com

ISBN: 978-1-913642-25-9

Contents

A Love Supreme
FRAGMENTS & EPHEMERA ... 7

The Music Does Not Matter
NOTES ON MUSIC IN LITERATURE ... 79

a song that would tell the story of all these things together
100 NOTES ON 3 ALBUMS ... 109

I'd sing you a song if I could sing
ART & ARTIFICE IN ELLEN DOUGLAS'S
   CAN'T QUIT YOU, BABY ... 135

Think Vertically!
NOTES FROM A COMP TEACHER'S DIARY ... 167

In Praise of Constraints
INCITING THE UNEXPECTED ... 183

One Take After Another
FRAGMENTS & EPHEMERA ... 195

Bibliography   241
Acknowledgments   255

To My Father

Once two birds got into the Rare Book Room.

—Jack Spicer

Sheets of Sound:
Notes on Music & Writing

───────────────

Jaydn DeWald

A Love Supreme
FRAGMENTS & EPHEMERA

My daughter likes a book called *Fancy Nancy's Favorite Fancy Words: From Accessories to Zany,* wherein each letter of the alphabet is represented by a "fancy" word that Nancy defines for the reader. For the letter "I," the word is "improvise"—"to use whatever is handy in order to make something."

*

In a workshop a few years ago, poet Dorianne Laux had each of her poet-students—five or six of us—tell the group how s/he had come to writing. I was pretty much the only student who hadn't read under a blanket every night as a child, gripping a flashlight. When my turn came, I said I came to literature late. (I didn't start reading books, much less writing poems or stories, until I was twenty and a student in community college.) When Dorianne asked what I did instead, I told her I played music. "Oh!" she said, throwing her hands in the air, as though I'd taken us on a long digression. "Same thing."

*

My first paid gig was a New Year's Eve ball at the McClellan Air Force Base with Milton Dick and his Orchestra. We played swing tunes for suited WWII veterans and their ball-gowned wives. Everybody in the "orchestra" was over sixty.

I was twelve. When I try to remember the event, I see my fellow musicians in tuxedoes; I see myself amongst them on the bandstand in blue- and white-striped pajamas—like one of the Darlings about to be swept off to Neverland—half petrified, half delirious merely to be up past my bedtime.

*

In "Memory as Melody," a review of Donald Justice's *The Sunset Maker* (1987), David St. John writes, "The formative experience of Justice's early instruction and acquaintanceship with music offers the axis upon which the book turns; it is the education of a sensibility that first learns the lessons of art and beauty in a medium other than words."

*

The most memorable poetry reading I ever attended wasn't, strictly speaking, a poetry reading at all, but rather a commemoration of the life and work of poet Stacy Doris, who had recently passed, at San Francisco State University. At one point—very touchingly—a number of her students stood at the four corners of the room, reading alternately to one another, call-and-response-style, *and* at the same time, like anarchic improvisers.

*

Like my students, I grow frustrated when the words—the ones worth keeping, anyway—drop onto the page with the weariness of a leaky faucet. I have to remind myself, as I have to remind them, that writing (no matter the speed) is not real-time composition. Not everybody's a precocious Menuhin, performing Bériot with the San Francisco Symphony Orchestra at age seven. Not every would-be artist goes to the crossroads and sells his or her soul to the devil.

*

In 1959, after hearing Ornette Coleman for the first time, Sonny Rollins decided he had to change his style, his very sound—he had to reestablish himself in contrast to Coleman—so he stopped gigging and practiced every day, all day, on the Williamsburg Bridge. After three years of seclusion, Rollins returned an entirely different player: quieter, more reserved, more patient. His so-called "comeback album" was called *The Bridge* (1962).

*

Magdalena Zurawski: "And the bridge when I looked up and saw it rising in the distance was less of a bridge now and more the symbol for loneliness."

*

In the beginning of Francis Ford Coppola's *The Conversation* (1974), Harry Caul, a surveillance man played by Gene Hackman, listening to a conversation he's been hired to record, says: "I don't care what they're talking about. All I want is a nice fat recording." Caul plays tenor sax in the film, but of course he plays only to jazz recordings: he would never play live; he would never let himself be surprised. He remains on the outside, a mere listener, a staunch nonparticipant. A real jazz musician—whatever that means exactly—would care very little about the recording, so long as what they're talking about could be heard (which is why, incidentally, most musicians are not audiophiles).

For all the meta-moments in the film—and there are many—I like best the final scene (spoiler alert) in which Caul, amidst his destroyed apartment wherein a "bug" has been planted, is playing his slightly out-of-tune tenor to the score of the film itself. Here, the emotional arc of Caul's character is completed not in language but in sound, in music: he finally acknowledges himself as—relinquishes himself to being—a character who can be heard, who can be listened to, and so breaks the proverbial fourth wall in the language of music.

*

Several weeks ago, one of my students, writing an essay on Dora Malech's "Love Poem," a poem in which the familiar words and emblems of love poetry (pet names, "forever," the moon) are playfully canted—"Tell me you'll dismember this night forever, / you my punch-drunking bag, tar to my feather"—came to my office for guidance. At the end of our conversation, I added (very much as an afterthought): "You might want to reckon with your title, too." A couple days later, he showed me a new draft. Significant attention had now been paid to Malech's own title, how it triggered particular expectations that the poem employs and subverts—

> More than the sum of our private parts, we are some
> peekaboo, some peak and valley, some
> bright equation (if *and* then *but*, if *er* then *uh*).
> My fruit bat, my gewgaw. You had me at *no duh*.

—so that the title is, finally, ironic, impersonal, comic (among other things). Having quite literally and cleverly taken my advice, the student had retitled his essay, "Reckon with the Title."

*

"[F]or better or worse," writes Junichiro Tanazaki, "we do love things that bear the marks of grime, soot, and weather, and we love the colors and the sheen that call to mind the past that made them."

*

Several nights ago, another pine tree toppled in our backyard—the third in five years—and now I'm out here watching my kids funambulate the trunk or rip clods of moss-laced dirt from its uprooted base. Unlike my garden-obsessed father, who I resemble in so many other ways (we're both jazz musicians, voracious novel-readers, diehard NBA fans, cognac enthusiasts, owners of lever-press espresso makers), I haven't once in five years worked to "improve" our half-acre backyard: its only discernible changes, frankly, are the stumps.

*

Musicians and writers and teachers are all well aware that their "work" is being spied upon. Indeed, the "success" of, say, a jazz performance or an essay or a lecture/discussion often depends on how well listeners or readers or students/administrators can spy upon it.

*

To believe one can teach anybody how to write in a single semester, a mere sixteen weeks—what hubris! I can only prod my students into the daily practice, the circadian motion, of writing; I can only encourage them to find a place—their own Williamsburg Bridge—to "play" without disturbance (or else with fruitful disturbance, as when a scrap of dialogue, overhead on a subway, squirms its way into a novel); and I can only put their writing in communication with the writing of their classmates or with the standards of excellence that line our bookshelves, a practice known among Zen Buddhists as "locking eyebrows."

*

In Benny Goodman's *The Famous 1938 Carnegie Hall Jazz Concert*, pianist Jess Stacy takes a remarkable, richly chorded solo. The story goes that, prior to the concert, Stacy had been listening to Debussy, and the great Impressionist pianist and composer still suffused his (sub)consciousness.

*

Wynton Marsalis once asked Stanley Crouch which jazz musicians could play the fastest. Crouch said: "Monk. Louis Armstrong. Ben Webster. Johnny Hodges." Wynton said: "But they don't play fast." "Yeah. But the thing is," Crouch replied, "you have a musical experience the moment you hear their sound. You can't play faster than that."

*

Marvin Bell, a former teacher of mine, believes writing is kinesthetic and metabolic. He writes late at night, sometimes all through the night, listening to French jazz radio, tapping his feet, verily bouncing (I imagine) in his desk chair. Occasionally, at some ungodly hour—musicians' hours, he might say—I'll receive from him an email with a link to a live online radio stream (Jazz Limoges France) accompanied by a single sentence like: "They're cooking tonight!" My students, many of them athletes and hikers and dancers and musicians, respond to such physicality. For them, half the difficulty of writing is the stationary-ness it requires: they equate writing with stillness of mind and body—and not "stillness" as mindfulness, either, but rather stillness as *stasis*—which, for most of us, most of the time, couldn't be further from the truth.

*

Writers, like jazz musicians, learn largely through osmosis.

*

sanctum sanctorum our windowless attic candlelit in which trembled my shadow our windowless attic walled round by records trembled my shadow stacks of spiral-bound fake books walled round by records there I sat under stacks of spiral-bound fake books in an outsized shirt there I sat under your brass galaxy of notes in an outsized shirt horn like a raised fist your brass galaxy of notes overhead shining horn like a raised fist running my fingers through dust overhead shining how could I be heard running my fingers through dust one rainy evening how could I be heard a dented tuba I found one rainy evening hugged it to my chest a pockmarked tuba I found with red cheeks ballooned hugged it to my chest blew a long low whale-like moan with red cheeks ballooned into the quiet blew a long low whale-like moan whereupon you turned into the quiet told me to *think vertically* whereupon you turned to your sheet music told me to *think vertically* or were you talking to your sheet music the rain snare-rolling the roof or were you talking my heart a doomed moth the rain snare-rolling the roof your horn upraising my heart a doomed moth candlelit in which I'm burning to hear you still sanctum sanctorum

*

A jazz record is a mass-produced artifact that can or will never be reproduced live. In general, the fan of pop music attends a pop concert in order to hear particular songs played in particular ways — that is to say, the way they are played on the radio—while the fan of jazz attends a jazz concert in order to hear particular musicians play what can never be played/heard again.

And even then the concert is sometimes not real or authentic enough. People who listened to Albert Ayler, the great free-jazz saxophonist, thought he was "out there," and he was. But in an episode of *The Trap Set with Joe Wong*, drummer Milford Graves, who played on Ayler's *Love Cry* (1968), claimed that the albums *and* the concerts were pretty tame: Ayler tamed himself so more people would listen, and because he wanted to make money. (Ayler "sold out" without selling out—a useful lesson for students no doubt—though for most writers and jazz musicians, the commerce of their art is frankly too laughable even to be called "commerce.") To really hear Ayler, Graves says, you had to hear him in private—at a private rehearsal, say, or while a club was closing down. "If you think you know who Ayler is," Graves says, "you are mistaken."

*

In a 2015 interview on KCRW's *Bookworm* with Michael Silverblatt, Mary Karr confessed to having thrown out twelve-hundred pages in her writing of *Lit* (2009). That's a lot of pages, but it doesn't shock, trouble or pain me. I played in a jazz quintet for over fifteen years, and I have—without any remorse or sorrow—no tangible evidence of having done so. Just experiences, just memories.

*

When I began teaching, I was blown away by the receptivity of my students. I was so used to being ignored, I *expected* to be ignored.

*

"Perhaps I like Louis Armstrong because he's made poetry out of being invisible," writes Ralph Ellison in *Invisible Man*. "And my own grasp of invisibility aids me to understand his music."

*

Each jazz concert is a unique performance, an artwork composed in real time. A writer reading his or her work is, on the whole, merely reciting—even most poetry readings are mere recitations—and therefore twice removed from real time: a live version of a pre-produced artwork that is itself pretending to be live. Yeats: "'A line may take us hours maybe; / Yet if it does not seem a moment's thought, / Our stitching and unstitching has been naught.'" I don't enjoy reading my work to an audience; I would much prefer to replace myself with a boom box, or better yet an old Edison cylinder phonograph (my grandmother, an antique dealer, had one), and just play a recording of my reading. I could even sit in the audience, head tilted, hands folded in my lap—that's how one's supposed to sit at a reading, isn't it?—completely and happily anonymous.

*

When Charlie Parker's name could not, for contractual reasons, appear on the cover of *Jazz at Massey Hall* (1953), he used the pseudonym "Charlie Chan"—a reference to the fictional detective *and* a gesture of love: his wife's nickname, the name by which everybody knew her, was Chan.

*

In the seventh grade, I was in a punk band called Hooligans Bound for Glory. Our first show was at a birthday party—a sunny Saturday afternoon. We set up in the birthday girl's backyard, on a large square of concrete, across from a folding table of juice and fruits and cookies and so forth, where a bunch of other seventh-graders had gathered. As our singer struggled to work a borrowed PA, and the guitarist and I tuned our instruments with coolly squinted eyes, a few boys shouted: *Come on! Play already! Show us what you got!*—and then, after another beat of silence, began to throw fruit at us. Well, the instant an orange slice struck his crash cymbal, our drummer said, "Fuck this, man," and immediately set to breaking down his kit. The rest of us—with almost comic rapidity—followed suit: we couldn't wait to get out of there. We were a horrible band, and not in a punk rock kind of way, either. When we "broke up" soon afterward, having never performed live even once, I felt only relief. Even our band name had been a shameful burden, a declaration to which I knew I could never live up.

*

Because personal writing can be difficult, I sometimes suggest my students give themselves pennames and write—however obliquely—to a specific addressee.

*

I understand the difficulty of writers, especially student writers, sharing their work. It's vulnerable, it's embarrassing, it's scary. To quote my friend d.: "people are mean and stupid and bad things happen." What's more, the writer is alone: the possibility of bonding through mutual, collective embarrassment is nonexistent. The only consolation is that the "performance" of the text occurs without the presence of the writer. For these reasons, I want the writing classroom to be a safe space, a place of encouragement and celebration and togetherness: everybody, even the teacher, is succeeding and failing and experimenting, and again failing and succeeding and failing and then experimenting again.

I have no patience at all for fruit-throwing.

*

ZERO HOUR, FOR ALL INSTRUMENTS

Storm Warning. Our garden crescendoes.
We weather changes like species of flies.
Play into the chord. Then break free of it.
The black cloud scats in contrary motion.
Our son's earlobes grow fat as bass clefs
And we clap. *Misty. God Bless the Child.*

I want to go acoustic with virtual fingers.
The phone become a seashell, the remote
Become a wand. On a pataphysical scale.
Giant Steps. Polka Dots and Moonbeams.
I see your range and raise you a half step.
We like to see the players' faces turn red.
Headline: *New York Licks Neo Bopsicles.*
Our marble fauns play a mean flute, man.

*

Historically, the livelihood of our great jazz musicians depended on playing live, which meant they might play three or fours hours a night. Despite market pressures, the necessity of playing live created an astonishing stew of creativity and innovation, and the status quo became very high indeed — a sociocultural situation that is, today (with the scarcity of jazz venues), largely nonexistent. In any event, such a situation could never occur among writers. Even in a world in which their livelihood depended on their reading before audiences, writers would simply be getting paid for *reading*, not for writing. In jazz, the work and the art are one and the same; in writing, the art is the product of the work. While writers would no doubt feel the significant pressure to write (in order to read) consistently new material, this pressure would not be nearly as generative or as innovational as the pressure of jazz musicians to play, to improvise before audiences. Unless you're David Antin, whose "talk poems" are, with uncommon skill and zest, composed extempore, writers composing on stage before a live audience would likely be boring performance art: a writer standing at a lectern, for instance, as Nabokov used to, as I am doing now, scribbling on notecards.

*

Improvisation, said pianist Billy Taylor, is "spontaneous composition based on the sense of form, content, and language of the song."

*

    6.26.56

    on a darkened road the leaden   clouds through bare trees the patter   of death against the windshield   a fingernail moon Nancy's   thin hands on the wheel a finger-   nail against the windshield   Brownie in the back & he   remembers   six years ago this June the crash the glass shattering he remembers   the double image the glass   shattering in synchronous blasts now the double black tires spinning   the past present future black   tires spinning the smoke of Richie's cigar   & the car   past present synchronous now the smoke curving round their heads &   round his contorted face as if "Embraceable You" he's playing "What Am I Here For?"   he remembers   the car lurching in the ruts & round & over the   embankment he's begun to play the rain the rain the patter of   death like   a record left spinning on a darkened road

*

At most jazz concerts, the audience is somewhat active: jazz, a physical art, elicits a physical response. Feet are tapping, heads are bobbing, eyes are darting from musician to musician (or are closed in bliss or concentration), and it's quite common to whoop or clap, which of course becomes part of the performance. Charles Mingus's albums in particular are filled with elated communal whooping and clapping. Just listen to *Mingus Ah Um* (1959)—possibly his greatest record—whose opening cut, "Better Git It in Your Soul," seems to have been recorded during a party.

*

Perhaps because writing is viewed as a "serious," solitary art, writing classrooms are all too often possessed with a stiff, reverential silence. As a teacher, I try to radiate zest and enthusiasm, and I love when students react audibly—a gasp or a laugh or an exclamatory "Wow!"—to the reading of a poem, say, or a short passage of an essay. My (pipe) dream is to make an entire class whoop and clap.

*

Keith Jarrett has for many years chastised his audiences for making even the slightest noise. Photographers and coughers are his sworn enemies.

*

Writers possess immense patience, a meditator's ability to focus on and seek out the fissures and potentialities of language, which may on the surface seem, however much the work attempts to engage the world, extraordinarily dull and hermetic, seeing as nothing but the quiet scratching of a pen, or the tapping of keys, can be observed. As Jack Gilbert writes in "Less Being More":

> It started when he was a young man
> and went to Italy. He climbed mountains,
> wanting to be a poet. But was troubled
> by what Dorothy Wordsworth wrote in
> her journal about William having worn
> himself out searching all day to find
> a simile for nightingale. It seemed
> a long way from the tug of passion.

*

Thelonious Monk was infamous for, at times, *not* playing. In one live footage from 1966, Monk stops playing around 2:15, and when the camera pans out about a minute later we see him tottering in circles, like a windup toy, staring down at his watch. Then, another minute later, he sits down again and begins to solo. Though Monk didn't dance at this particular concert, it was quite common for him to get up, right out of the blue, and start dancing, too.

*

Specialized music and writing are like cultures that require some acclimatization.

*

Well-known Dizzy quote: "It's taken me all my life to learn what not to play."

*

At the 2002 Concert for George, Ravi Shankar (whose improvisatory ragas might be an Indian, centuries-old equivalent to jazz) sat down on stage and began to tune his sitar. When he was finished tuning, he received a hearty applause. Only slowly did he realize that this American audience all believed he had just performed a song.

*

If my students want to climb mountains in search of similes, I will not object. But because most of my students—or, frankly, most *people*—are quite uninterested in simile-questing, I try to convince them that writers are armchair voyagers and that some experiences can in fact only be had on the page, with or in or through language—a lot of passion-tugging indeed—and that these, too, are real experiences, *real events* to remember or forget, and arguably more peculiar or individual than experiences in so-called "real life" as well, since nobody else can experience them.

*

My father had on vinyl Miles' *My Funny Valentine* (1964)—a terrific live album recorded at the Philharmonic Hall (now the David Geffen Hall) in New York City. But it was an old copy, warped from neglect, and it skipped a few bars into the title track's remarkable intro. One night, alone, when my girlfriend was supposed to meet me at my house—this was my freshman year in high school—I decided I wanted her to discover me in the dark, listening to this album. It would be so romantic, wouldn't it? I imagined she would appear like Grace Kelly in *Rear Window*—a shadow looming over me—and kiss me, a teenaged Jimmy Stewart, as I lay on the couch. Because the record skipped, however, I had to get up every two-and-a-half-minutes, turn on a lamp, and, lowering the needle carefully into the groove, start the record all over again—a little Sisyphean procedure I repeated (embarrassingly) too many times to count.

When she arrived at last, my girlfriend flicked on every light leading to our living room, calling out over the music: "Where are you? Why the hell's it so dark in here?"

*

If Marvin Bell is right, and "originality is just a new amalgam of influences," as he once told me in a letter, then the influences a group of jazz musicians—as well as a classroom of students—brings to the aesthetic/intellectual table is enormous. An amalgamation indeed.

*

So much of the "teaching" of writing—perhaps even the teaching of art in general—lies in sharing experiences and anecdotes. I want my students to feel that we're all in this together, that our frustrations and ambitions can be dealt with, at least in part, collectively, and that all these conversations color our individual experiences of "making."

*

Elizabeth Hardwick: "To proceed from musing to writing is to feel a robbery has taken place. And certainly there has been a loss; the loss of the smiles and ramblings and discussions so much friendlier to ambition than the cold hardship of writing."

*

In Juzo Itami's *Tampopo* (1985), the central plot is intermittently interrupted with gastronomic comedy sketches. In one such interruption, a white-suited gangster pauses in the middle of a kiss with his lover to crack an egg, drain the albumen, and tip the raw yolk from its light brown half-shell into his mouth. Then he and his lover commence to slide the yolk back and forth from each other's mouths until, in deathlike ecstasy, the woman orgasms, goes limp, and the yolk runs like yellow blood or cum from the corners of her mouth.

*

On the title track of *Milestones* (1958), the soloists are conjoined (the last phrase of one soloist is repeated, with slight variation, in the opening phrase of the subsequent soloist) like a crown of sonnets.

*

Can we, reader and writer, slide together like bright yolk from vignette (mouth) to vignette (mouth)? Will there be — doubtful — a climactic orgasm?

*

Because we encounter language relentlessly in a variety of media, as well as in common speech, I suspect the layperson is more openly skeptical of — less willing to entertain — what might be called "specialized" or "difficult" writing, such as theory or criticism or poetry (which refutes, cants, or in someway intellectually or artfully employs ordinary speech) than of jazz (which, being music, is "other" enough to politely tolerate at a distance). Doesn't every Hollywood cocktail party have a tuxedoed, West Coast-style combo playing a little too quietly in the corner?

*

There's a wonderful scene in Julian Schnabel's 1996 biopic *Basquiat*. Miles' "Flamenco Sketches" is playing — a haunting ballad, Bill Evans on the keys — and Jean-Michele Basquiat (Jeffrey Wright) walks at night down a New York street and then through a crowd and into his first gallery show, where a greasy-haired twenty-something removes his headphones, and the music is at once replaced with the babble of the art crowd.

To which universe does Basquiat (and viewers) belong — the private world of art, or the public world of art commerce?

*

Oh, students, I beg you not to play quietly in the corner.

*

Last weekend, I asked my partner, Kali: "What do you think about when you think about jazz?" We were driving through humid green Georgia countryside, so that our three-year-old daughter would take a nap, and so that Kali could spot "dream houses." She's found a thousand dream houses in Athens alone, and she uses each house as a pretext for talking about the future with me (who tends not to see beyond the tip of his nose). She's the most beautiful woman on the planet. Anyway, distracted, craning her neck to better see a lemon-yellow barn-style house with a wraparound porch, she answered: "Intellectuals with money."

*

For all his desire and ability to sell records, Miles — perpetual *Rückenfigur* — would never stop turning his back on his audience. Because of Miles, I allow students to turn their back on me, their "audience": I feel it is their artistic and/or temperamental right.

*

THE ONE TIME I SAW MONK
PLAYING AT MINTON'S

He looked like a drunk hammering on a typewriter. Me and Corwell in gray silk suits, black-on-black shirts, and Butcher Boys shoes. Cigars and whiskies and little hotties on our shoulders. Did his "angular rhythms clash like gods in the smoke overhead?" Come on, kid, I wasn't even listening.

*

Writers tend to give readings so that you will read their books; they are, on the whole, promoting their work. Jazz musicians invert this equation: they cut records so that you will attend their concerts—the real art is played live, in the clubs, and the record is mostly a promotional tool and a status symbol. This is partly an inherent quality of the spirit of jazz—improvisatory, communal, determinedly non-reproducible. Yet it's also partly a means of self-protection and of art preservation. Until only recently, record labels exploited jazz musicians outright: musicians got paid very little for cutting records (often needing money to support a drug addiction) and many never owned them, either, not even infinitesimally, which is just to say musicians and their families never received any royalty checks. According to musician and jazz scholar

Gordon Vernick, labels like Blue Note, which produced many of our most celebrated albums, continue to rerelease old records in new editions simply because they needn't pay anybody a penny.

*

A few years ago, my father and I were hired by Martin B. (I won't reveal his surname)—a crooner who should have been born a century ago—to play a gig at a Chinese restaurant in Sacramento. We arrive at a banquet-style place filled with streamers and glitter—it was some sort of Chinese cultural/political gathering—and everybody's dressed to the nines. Except for us, of course, because Martin failed to mention that this was a black-tie affair. He tells us to set up in a little cramped corner by the door. Meanwhile, on the big stage, a Chinese pop group from Hollywood is practicing. Their singer looks like a Chinese Joan Didion: very small and chic, huge dark sunglasses. Although we were hired to play from six to seven, this group practices until six-thirty. So we just sit there for a half-hour while Martin arranges his business cards and demo CDs on a folding table, and goes around vigorously shaking hands with everybody. Then we begin. He calls up "A Sleepin' Bee"—the Mel Torme version. Long story short, halfway through our third tune, we get cut off by the Flower Drum Song and a dancing dragon, and are told to pack it up. Martin had apparently offered us up for free, hoping (I can only guess) to get discovered. The poor guy's always trying to get "discovered." He paid everybody out of his own pocket. Four hundred dollars for two-and-a-half tunes. I felt bad for him, but I'd driven all the way from San Francisco to play the gig, so of course I took the money.

I got paid as a musician without being a musician, for merely "performing," as it were, the practical routine of traveling and dressing up, of lugging around an instrument and an amp.

*

Just as Richard A. Lanham wants to include business savvy as part of the art of Christo and Jean-Claude's *Running Fence* (1967), a 24.5-mile veiled fence running across the deer-tan hills of Sonoma and Marin—"no greater monument to business entrepreneurship has ever been erected," Lanham writes—so I want to include business indifference as part of the art of jazz and writing and teaching.

*

I imagine some evil capitalist Professor X entering Cerebro and donning the metallic helmet that allows him to see—well, not mutants, as in the X-Men comics, but moneymakers, earners. I sleep soundly knowing the poets will never be found.

*

One of my early writing teachers had a humungous handwritten sign taped to his office door: ASS IN CHAIR! Though students won't get credit for the practical routine of sitting at their desks with pens and paper, I still feel this act is worth something. And it is: Students often tell me they feel accomplished after writing their name, or giving their essay a title, or including the requisite works cited page, and they sometimes—almost by accident—begin to write in earnest, feeling perhaps that the foundational or most tiresome part of the writing process has been completed.

*

It has always seemed to me an advantage that poetry—the genre in which I'm most comfortable (or productively uncomfortable) and which informs my approach to the teaching of composition—has little to no monetary value, or use value, either, that it's basically free from market pressures: it pushes back, albeit softly, against Guy Debord's spectacle. To receive money for poetry might dangerously, to quote Natalia Ginzburg, "implicitly affirm the principle—a false one—that money is the crowning reward for work, its ultimate objective."

*

In Alan Hollinghurst's novel *The Spell* (1998), a young protagonist named Alex goes to a club and takes Ecstasy for the first time. After a while, "it seemed [to Alex] that happening and happiness were the same." Is that the ultimate goal of jazz— to make happening and happiness the same? No: not merely *happiness*, but rather the entire spectrum of potential emotions. By attempting to reinvent itself moment-to-moment, jazz synchronizes happening and any number of emotions.

Most texts are created likewise, moment-to-moment; the difference is that a text, in a reader's hands, cannot be changed. This is why the language(s) of my favorite texts are multifaceted, prismatic, pluralistic: they induce in readers a seemingly inexhaustible variety of interpretations, perspectives, and emotions all at the same time.

*

Once, as kids, my sister (who kept a diary and liked to read and write) handed our father a sheet of paper on which she'd written a poem. My father gushed over it, embraced her, couldn't believe she'd written something so beautiful. I (who hated reading and writing) watched this little scene and thought, "Damn. I want that hug." So I carried our *Webster's Dictionary* into my room and wrote a poem composed entirely of ginormous words I'd never heard of before. Minutes later, I strutted into the living room and handed Dad my poem. He read it. Squinting. Looking from me to the poem and then back to me again. Tentatively he said: "I don't think you know what you're talking about."

To everybody's surprise, my sister is now a professional bodybuilder, and I'm a poet.

*

As a musician—an electric bassist—I felt from the beginning the urge to disappear. I loved, *still* love, playing live, which is of course a kind of disappearing act: you escape into the world of music, even as you and your music both remain perceptible to the phenomenal world. But then the tune's over, and you're back on stage, or on a large square of concrete, or in the corner of a marble-floored Italian restaurant, or under a purple, sun-brightened tent in front of a winery in . . . where are you again?

*

I don't rush student writing toward "neatness," "polishing," "finishing," etc, etc, which has always struck me as a cruelty. Imagine a friendship in which one person is always ready and willing to embalm the other. Quite to the contrary, I try to convince my students to keep their texts (via revision, rearrangement, reconsideration, reflection, resistance—all those valuable *re-* words) alive and communicative, for as long as possible, because at a certain point (the due date?) the text must be, if not finished, as Valéry famously said, then abandoned.

*

In music and writing, I welcome disappearance. In teaching, however, I have to remember that there are real people in front of or beside or all around me, and I have to communicate with them—get them to communicate with each other—not merely as sound or as language, but as a human being.

*

My feeling is that jazz wants to be made privately (even if collaboratively)—like an after-hours Ayler concert—but the medium denies it: one cannot make music without sound, a sensory perception open, so to speak, to the public. "There is no way to stop sound and have sound," said Walter J. Ong. This inherent conflict (the publicness of music and the privacy of artistic expression) can be a generative creative force. In a single concert, a musician, even an entire band, can play *to*, *for* and *against* his or her audience.

For student writers, a classroom of healthy or fraught discussions, lively or restrained debate, creates audiences, even if for just one semester. Consciously or un-, students also begin to write to and for and against their peers.

*

These two disciplines, music and writing, are not elitist. Practitioners do not purposefully obfuscate their material for their own amusement or haughty avant-gardism, as though they like to see laypeople scratch their heads. Music and writing are instead like dialects, or interrelated groups of dialects, which is complicated further by a deep investment in individuality, in each artist finding his or her "voice" within and in opposition to the prevailing dialects."

*

Ellen Douglas: "It just occurred to me, I might include an additional challenge, the element of a puzzle: Which episode goes where?"

EVENING SKETCHES: AFTER C.D. WRIGHT

the river   the fire   the music   the hour   the attic   the water

the forest   the naming   the dragon   the curtain   the moonlit   the hour

the rainstorm   the spires   the dragon   the eyelid   the blossom   the scatter

the footprint   the rapture   the dragon   the shadow   the nocturne   the fever

the shadow   the mother   the body   the naming   the beetle   the shifting

the double   the octave   the eyelid   the rising   the nocturne   the rapture

the river   the spires   the attic   the fire   the footprint   the hour   the curtain   the water

the blossom   the octave   the rainstorm   the scatter   the moonlit

the rapture   the shadow   the fire   the nocturne   the fever   the music

the cunning   the forest   the dragon   the body   the naming   the shadow

the mother   the octave   the beetle   the curtain   the shifting

the music   the fire   the double   the octave   the river   the rising

*

As a student at Sacramento City College, my father wrote a composition for Jazz Band called "LSD 67," which consisted of a series of unconnected melodies and musical ideas (stacked fourths; dense, atonal chord clusters; angular percussion and brass; a whole lot of communal improvisation) gathered haphazardly together and bookended with musicians breathing—as though exhausted—into their mouthpieces. After its debut at the '67 Reno Jazz Festival, one friend commented: "Well, it does sound like a bad trip."

*

The compositional strategies of these fragments are, I believe, a response to my father's early music.

*

Text and music maintain different relationships to time. Even though some of the most beautiful and surprising writerly moments arise from the pressure of real-time composition, texts are largely attempts to stop time—"the dream of all poetry, to cut a hole in time" (Mary Ruefle)—whereas music attempts to embody time, to be one with time, for time to coarse through one's lips or lungs, one's throat or fingertips. When time stops, music stops.

*

On my worst teaching days, I am like the title character of Andrei Tarkovsky's *Stalker* (1979) upon his disconsolate return from The Zone: "Their eyes are blank." (Sobbing.) "Nobody believes." His wife puts him to bed, gives him a sleeping pill, and wipes the sweat and tears from his face.

*

About jazz. About jazz musicians. In my view, most so-called "jazz poetry" is *about* jazz and jazz musicians, as opposed to approaching writing improvisationally or emulating in language the technical features of jazz (swing or syncopation, for example). Though there are significant exceptions, the bulk of such writing is merely written with apparent looseness: it seems to insist on rhythmic irregularity; their lines tend to be elastic; neologisms abound (e.g. "parkerflights," from Bob Kaufman's "On"); scat-like phrases frequently appear ("Pitter patter, boom dropping" from Kaufman's "O-Jazz-O," or "doo doot doo Where is Dick Gallup" from Ted Berrigan's "String of Pearls"). This kind of jazz poetry can be extraordinary, and I find Kaufman's work in particular profound. Still, the technical features of this writing is very rarely akin to the technical features of jazz, because the latter relies too heavily upon tempo and key, music's inbuilt (or, more likely, *ingrained*) expectations. Jazz is built upon the antagonization or swerving of expectations, and though jazz poetry does indeed swerve from more traditional poetry, whose compositional decisions are based on meter or syllabics or stanzaic patterning, they nevertheless establish themselves as regularly irregular, predictably unpredictable. Whereas a jazz tune attempts to break the expectations established by the tune itself, "jazz poetry" attempts to break the expectations of poetry *in general*.

*

There's another wonderful scene early in *Basquiat*. Benny Dalmau (Benicio del Toro) is showing Jean-Michel a makeshift music video of one of their band's songs. Jean-Michel mutes the television, and Benny says: "What, you don't like it with the music?"

"I like it like this," says Basquiat.

On the screen: a black-and-white, stop-action sequence of a man prancing down a sidewalk toward the camera.

"It's boring like this," Benny replies. "Like—it's—. It's like looking at a painting. You need music. You need sound."

Of course, in the context of the film, this reveals Basquiat's artistic sensibility and foreshadows his greatness as a painter. But the scene also excites me because the viewer confronts this aesthetic quandary, too, and may feel very differently. I, for instance, despite my love for visual art, always want to turn off the hyperactive video and simply listen to the music, which has a nice funky bassline.

*

A tune is in fact innumerable tunes with the same title. Put another way, the jazz tune is—like a canvas in an action painting—the arena in which works of art collide.

*

EVENING SKETCHES: AFTER RONALD PERRY

Concert's over	*Tunes forgotten*
Houselights dimming	*Birds and darkness*
Cymbals ringing	*Till tomorrow*
On and on.	*Nothing lost.*

Fingers tired
  Spider dancing
Forward backward
  Like a heart.

After midnight
  Mind on fire
Crowd dispersing
  Into cars.
Cold November
  Walking solo
Down a side street
  Like a bass.

All musicians
  (Poets know this)
Covet silence
  As a sound.
Buzzing neon
  Storefront windows
Ghost reflections
  Floating where

Staves of shadow
  Throb the sidewalk
Arc lamps flicker
  Snowflakes fall.
Who still hears us
  Without axes
Trailing music
  In green air?

What do notes mean
  Stone and tulip
Facing inward
  Bursting out?

Ink on parchment
  "Winter Sunset"
Crooners' lovers
  Make no sound.
Scent of coffee
  Wind in alleys
Blue it floated
  Phantom ur-.

Contrapuntal
  Double solo
Bodies pressing
  Skin to skin.
Tunes remembered
  Octaves stacking
Starless moonless
  Overhead.

Minor changes
  Forward backward
Haunt the nightscape
  New flâneur.
Path of bootprints
  Under bridges
Strewn with garbage
  Like a chord.

*

Ellen Bryant Voigt: "A great jazz musician needs a group, a trio, a partner instrument to maintain the ghost of the pulse against which the idiosyncratic improvisations can occur. It is the counterpoint we respond to."

*

How can writing and music be combined, or even talked about, without producing this effect, this desire to choose one discipline over another? I'm not sure I have an answer. Yet the desire *not* to choose is in part this essay's *raison d'être*, and indeed creative writing and composition studies incorporates, champions even, multimodality more and more. Though admittedly less multimodal than cross-disciplinary, my own writing, and therefore my approach to the teaching of writing, is far more indebted to my experiences in and knowledge of music (jazz in particular) than to the experience in and knowledge of writing proper.

*

Suzan-Lori Parks: "'Repetition and Revision' is a concept integral to the Jazz esthetic in which the composer or performer will write or play a musical phrase once and again and again; etc.—with each revisit the phrase is slightly revised. 'Rep & Rev' as I call it is a central element in my work; through its use I'm working to create a dramatic text that departs from the traditional linear narrative style to look and sound more like a musical score."

*

Most of my students presume that the writing produced in college should be—strives to be—intelligently impersonal, dictatorially controlled. They don't realize that the writing of both students and professors often "use mistakes," as Picasso asserted, or "deny mistakes," as Pollock (revising Picasso) claimed. They don't realize that engagement with the world, however clumsy or arbitrary or angular it may be, is inescapably personal and, as in jazz, as in stage acting, as in sports, as in interpersonal relationships (this list could go on and on), it requires significant in-the-moment collaboration/improvisation.

*

Stephen Crane once sent "[a] monocled Englishman named Bassett Holmes"—I'm quoting from John Berryman's 1950 critical biography of Stephen Crane—a copy of his *Maggie*, with this memorable note: "This work is a mud-puddle, I am told on the best authority. Wade in and have a swim."

*

Writing is not a wholly non-improvised art, even if it is in this regard, compared to jazz, rather tame. I once heard a story—who knows if it's true?—about James Joyce writing *Ulysses*. Beckett was taking dictation, because Joyce was by then as blind as a mole, and during a particularly intense compositional moment—he was "writing" at quite a clip—there came a knock at the door. Joyce, without pause, said: "Get the door," so Beckett asked: "Do you want me to get the door, or do you want me to write, 'Get the door'?" Instantly Joyce barked: "Both!"

*

Last semester, I had a student who had been riding and boarding horses since she was a little girl, and I could tell in her prose how much care and attention, how much *work*, she put into many of her paragraphs, which no doubt sprung in part from the ritual of stepping into her boots and lumbering in the predawn dark toward her barn, where she would feed, brush, bathe, and saddle her horses. She also knew, almost intuitively, how and when to simply ride the language, to let language—itself a smooth muscular fast-running animal—carry her from here to there. "As I walk into the white, steep-pitched barn," she wrote in one essay, "I am greeted by the distinct smell of hay and straw and manure and soap and lemon oil and leather and old brick and wood and time."

*

Geoffrey Sirc: "A primary goal now in my writing classes: to show my students how their compositional future is assured if they take an art stance to the everyday, suffusing the materiality of daily life with an aesthetic."

*

I began to skateboard when I was eleven or twelve years old, and I worked at it the way other kids ran scrimmages or went to the batting cages or rehearsed an after-school production of *Macbeth*. Though it was almost always fun—my friends and I wouldn't have skated every day until dark or later, risking punishment, if it wasn't fun—skating nevertheless requires a lot of practice, patience, determination, resilience, stubbornness, guts (among many other things), even though none of us was ever quite good enough. Then again, no skater worth his or her salt *is* ever quite good enough: there seems to be a principle of failure built into the practice. That's why most skate videos have "fall sections" (montages of hard, sometimes brutal spills), why even our best skaters very frequently fall or "bail" (abandon the board mid-trick), and why I wasn't pissed at my dad for asking one afternoon, after he'd stood around for a while stroking his mustache, pursing his lips, watching a bunch of us skate a launch ramp and a knee-high box: "Don't you guys ever get tired of messing up?" I knew this question, never mind its indelicate phrasing, was an attempt to understand the general practice of skateboarding—and even now, some seventeen years later, I can think of no truer response than the terse one I'd given him. "Skating's hard, Dad."

*

"Spend a full 8-hour day on a skateboard and see if, by the end of it, you ollie an inch high or even skillfully maneuver around the streets," writes Jeff Alessandrelli in *Biggie Smalls Skateboarding Superstar*. "Don't be surprised if you can't come close."

*

Those who say they don't understand jazz or specialized writing have not been exposed to them deeply enough. They are expecting these disciplines to be accessible, general, transparent—to speak *to* them, in short, like pop music or a car manual. Instead, both disciplines simply speak in their own languages, and what happens afterward, in the domain of the general public, as opposed to the domain of enthusiasts/practitioners, is either *fortunate* (your book wins a Pulitzer; your record goes platinum) or *unfortunate* (your book gets banned or burned or taken to court for obscenity; you get beaten up outside an LA club, like Ornette Coleman).

*

Students sometimes think my views on writing are prescriptive, that I'm looking for some particular brand of "difficult" writing. This couldn't be further from the truth. On the spectrum ranging from, say, total obfuscation to depthless accessibility, there is so much room to play; I merely prefer, aesthetically and intellectually, writing that challenges both reader and writer—writing that, like jazz, struggles with itself as it progresses.

*

Will Self: "After all, one of the great things about writing, as opposed to other media, is that it makes no claims on people unless they engage with it: words, no matter how torturous, don't leap out of books and articles and assault you."

*

Isn't oblivion the ultimate unfortunateness? Perhaps for most writers the answer is resoundingly yes, seeing as the posterity of his or her work largely depends on reprinting: the reprinting of individual books, the reprinting of one's collected work (we should be so lucky), and perhaps especially the anthologizing of individual, so-called "representative" essays or poems or short stories. Jazz, however, is an ephemeral art, which is just to say that jazz musicians live with oblivion every night: the work is produced (via a concert) and never heard again, even if it lives on in the unreliable memories of listeners and musicians. For writers, the act of making a text is ephemeral, whereas the text itself has, one hopes, a long(er) shelf life. I do not lament the ephemerality of writing—after all, I can at any moment simply write something new—but instead feel rather contemptuous of my own "finished" texts, which are now separate from me, which have (as set-in-stone artifacts) turned me, the writer, into a reader-voyeur, and which have the potential, however unlikely, to go on without me. As a former jazz musician, I am quite comfortable with oblivion: it doesn't seem to me the most unfortunate public response to one's work at all, seeing as it doesn't even involve the practitioner, who can simply continue (unlike an imprisoned artist, such as Ai Wei Wei) to compose, to make, to "play."

*

Marvin Bell once told me that Robert Creeley—at a small private poetry reading in New York City, in the mid-1960s—read the same poem again and again, intent on reciting its rhythms precisely. For a time, there was in the poetry community a somewhat contentious argument (very bizarre, in my view) over the validity of pausing at the ends of lines, which Creeley and Denise Levertov and many other terrific poets believed in. Years later—at the Kelly Writers House in 2000—Creeley would bring to a public discussion about his work a now-primitive computer program that could read a text on a word processor aloud. He seemed proud to have finally obtained objective proof about the matter: the robotic voice reciting one of his poems clearly paused at the ends of lines.

*

After reading a recent work of mine, one writer friend told me that, because of its punctuation, he felt like a passenger in a truck whose driver was just learning stick.

*

TO MY TEACHER

your hand on my   hand in my living room   alone
ghosting this pencil over lined paper   in my living
room alone   the air's electric over lined   paper

    & faintly as in half-sleep   the air's electric your
cornet erupts & faintly as in half-   sleep tearing
through silence   your cornet erupts so that I stand
inside it   tearing through silence incorporeal so
that I stand inside it a legato wail in-   corporeal
translated to leaden words a legato wail *a boy on a boat*
translated to leaden words except   you're here *a*
boy on a boat the sound   of your bodymind except
you're here with me   on the page the sound of
your body-   mind walking in circles with me on
the page is an orange-blue bowl   of sky walking in
circles in robe & sockfeet is an orange-   blue bowl
of sky now we can grow large in   robe & sockfeet
with my distorted sitar now   we can grow large I
call out to you with my dis-   torted sitar the notes
between notes I feed-   back to you a shadow uncoupling the notes be-   tween notes across your
table a shadow uncoupling   kaleidoscopic across
your table   your own grid-paper notebook kaleidoscopic galaxy of words   ghosting this pencil your
own grid-paper notebook galaxy   of words toward
which I reach &   reach my   hand on your hand

*

My students are always talking about "flow." They want their texts to *flow*. Good flow, they believe, means good writing. There's some truth to this: if readers have to reread every other sentence, as a result of clumsy phrasing or grammatical no-nos, then there's usually some work to be done. Still, a text that requires no rereading, a text whose every phrase bleeds seamlessly into the next, tends to be too safe or superficial or tidy. No struggle to speak of.

*

In music, syncopation refers to rhythmic displacement—placing beats or accents unexpectedly—which of course relies upon rhythmic regularity: one can only play "off" if playing "on" has been established. A jazz soloist tends to syncopate against the steady downbeats of a drummer's ride cymbal and/or a bassist's walking. So how does one syncopate in his or her writing, which is, so to speak, a solo performance? In my view, to syncopate in a text is to syncopate against that text's rhythmic expectations, and the commonest way to establish rhythmic expectations is to simply write in received forms. Let us examine briefly the poetry of Shane McCrae, for example, who almost always transforms received forms via rhythmic displacement, what might be called "poetic syncopation."

Nearly every poem in McCrae's debut collection, *Mule* (2011), is a sonnet or a series of sonnets, and though these sonnets are in many ways straightforward—they're iambic, they consist of 70 beats, they often rhyme and posses a volta—they don't look at all like sonnets:

Horses Running Fast

We married in an open field a wide
And open field a field of wild and run- / ning
horses wide a field of horses run- / ning through
we married in an open wide
Running and full   of horses open
field / And in we married in   and in we mar- / ried in in
one direction they the hors- / es they
disguised the wind as horses in the wind / The horses running
fast in one / Direction
as the horses running through   / The horses as the horses
run- / ning through
and each of us as me and you / As horses running fast
In one direction and
no animal outruns its past

By shattering the sonnet's typical appearance with caesuras and virgules (as well as by disregarding a sonnet's somewhat arbitrary necessity to be fourteen lines), McCrae allows himself to syncopate against the metrical regularity of a sonnet: the poem's virgules indicate the line breaks of the sonnet proper, and the majority of the actual line breaks, along with the caesuras, are experienced as syncopation, unexpected accents and pauses, over and against the sonnet's rhythmic expectations (iambic pentameter). In other words, the perceptive, sonnet-savvy reader will feel—at the virgule—that he or she has moved, or ought to have moved, to the next line, even though the line continues. This is an effect enhanced, moreover, by McCrae's use of repetition:

the poem is always moving forward even as it fractures itself and returns to a former compositional moment. In this way, "Horses Running Fast," which is formally indicative of McCrae's work in general, has become a field—"an open field a wide / And open field"—wherein regularized sound and sense (fourteen lines doled out in iambic pentameter, without his backstitch-like repetition) combat peculiar, seemingly improvisatory syncopation and repetition.

*

Punctuation, paragraph breaks, section breaks, line breaks, caesuras, virgules, etc., etc.—all of these are, in a sense, rhythmic notation: they attempt, among other things, to objectivize a text's pauses and emphases. Even so, every text remains, for good or for ill, susceptible to the idiosyncrasies of a given reader, whose natural cadences or respiratory rhythm or sense of pause-for-effect will likely differ from the writer's. Not such a big deal. After all, even the most formal of poems, the most rhythmically controlled writing I can think of, would be very awkward indeed if read "perfectly"—to a metronome, say. And would we then also supply texts with time signatures and tempos? No, these seem to me distracting accoutrements, and most formal poems aspire for naturalness, anyway, so that its sound and its content are experienced as a single, inseparable entity. (Auden's "As I Walked Out One Evening," naturally read in 4/4, can be read in any other time signature, too: the accents (emphases) merely fall on—the pauses merely fall between—different words or syllables that do not reflect the poem's abovementioned rhythmic notation.) Like, say, Michael Brecker playing "Naima," solo, the "tempo" of a text (that is, the expectations established by its general rhythmic characteristics) tends to be fairly elastic. Thus, even if readers are merely witness to an event in language, the act of reading/witnessing—to say nothing of content—is significantly individual.

*

Adorno: "Even the creations of phantasy that are supposedly independent of time and space, point toward individual existence—however far they may be removed from it."

*

Writing this essay, if indeed it is an essay, I keep thinking of Bernard Malamud's short story "Pictures of an Artist," wherein the protagonist, the artist Arthur Fidelman, travels from place to place digging holes, "a succession of spontaneously placed holes, each a perfect square, which when seen together constituted a sculpture." An ominous association, of course, since Fidelman is later visited by a stranger described rather like the reaper "wrapped in the folds of a heavy cloak" who soon "smote[s]" Fidelman with his own shovel, "a resounding blow on the head, the sculptor toppling as though dead into the larger of the two holes he himself had dug."

*

For street skaters, a "line" is a series of consecutive tricks—a "succession of spontaneously placed holes"—the kind of skateboarding Whitmanians will admire.

*

> when he appeared there before the hole in the ground a summer evening he held out to me before the hole in the ground my rosebud skateboard he held out to me distortion & power chords my rosebud skateboard so like two night trains distortion & power chords side by side we rode like two night trains so stems resprouted in my heart side by side we rode through desolate streets in my heart stems resprouted consecutive tricks through desolate streets known in skating as a line consecutive tricks a call & response known in skating as a line into our past a call & response under flicking lamplight into our past our boards echo under sodium streetlight then I reached for him our boards echo to touch his face once again then I reached for him slowly through still air once again to touch his face my hand pushed through him through still air slowly a reverse cymbal sounding pushed my hand through him forward I tumbled a reverse cymbal sounding & thumped to the ground I tumbled forward among frightwigs of dead grass & thumped to the ground his name on my lips among frightwigs of dead grass the dark of the hole his name on my lips a summer evening I can never stop replaying when he appeared there

*

Do readers personalize texts sonically, the way jazz musicians personalize melodies? For the reader, a personalized "melody" would necessitate the replacing of words, the shifting of clauses, perhaps some idiosyncratic cutting or expanding—ultimately destroying the autonomy of the text by ignoring its implicit singularity. Then again, sometimes, when a student reads a text aloud for the class, s/he will bestow it with a cadence, a real music, that was not at all apparent to me on the page.

*

Where am I? Have I lost the thread?

In Itami's *The Last Dance* (1993), the protagonist, a terminally ill film director, attempts suicide, at which point his spirit is ejected from his body and, tethered by an ethereal red thread, floats above it, like a balloon. When a doctor's arm snaps the thread, the director's spirit soars vertiginously through a Carrollian rabbit hole and then experiences—or do only viewers experience?—a surrealist montage of collagelike images. One moment the director is tearing the skin back from his cheek to reveal yellow corn; the next, popcorn is geysering out of his disappearing skull.

It turns out my favorite moment in the film is when the director has, as it were, lost the thread.

*

On the old ten-inch 78s, a tune could be no longer than three or so minutes; consequently, jazz musicians sometimes shortened heads (or omitted them altogether) in order to lengthen their solos.

*

A "head" is a tune's primary theme or melody, with its corresponding chord progression. The head establishes, for soloists, the harmonic vocabulary and rhythmic expectations, though almost every worthy solo stretches a tune's harmonic vocabulary and challenges its rhythmic expectations. For many jazz musicians and enthusiasts, the head is the most expendable appendage.

*

> a minor earthquake rattling pills & teacups bolt upright we were under moon-white sheets rattling pills & teacups unable to sleep under moon-white sheets naked you & I swapped dreams unable to sleep you sat at a desk naked you & I swapped dreams an empty classroom you sat at a desk on the wall a silent film an empty classroom alice a study on the wall a silent film a narrow mud hole alice a study trapped among worms & beetles a narrow mud hole huge insectile eyes trapped among worms & beetles mascara black tears huge insectile eyes thrashing hair in fast-forward mascara black tears gushing like black veins thrashing

hair in fast-forward & in the meantime gushing like black veins my apartment on fire & in the meantime I ran round & round my apartment on fire applause & strobelight I ran round & round a massive pile of trash applause & strobelight as in a gameshow a massive pile of trash doll-like shadows flung as in a gameshow I can save one possession doll-like shadows flung on torn wallpaper I can save one possession this used orange teabag on torn wallpaper or single-tusked stuffed walrus this used orange teabag whereupon silence or velvet-tongued stuffed walrus leaked across the room whereupon silence still neither of us could sleep leaked across the room & I didn't breathe still neither of us could sleep bolt upright we were & I didn't breathe waiting under moon-white sheets for you to touch me a minor earthquake

*

Lisa Robertson: "This object furnishes hospitable conditions for entering and tarrying; it shelters without fastening; it conditions without determining." Pretty good definition of a fake book. Pretty good definition of my student's in-progress essays, too.

*

Sharon Crowley: "[C]omposition is primarily a productive or generative art rather than an analytical or interpretive one."

*

In "Isle of Java," from Jackie McLean's *Jackie's Bag* (1960), tenor saxophonist Tina Brooks plays "Mary had a Little Lamb" in the middle of his solo, though of course he plays it "out"—a half-step sharp, if memory serves—so it's hip, not cutsey. McLean makes Western European children's music sound very hip indeed.

*

Is Brooks' dissonant "Mary had a Little Lamb" all that different from Dora Malech "dismember[ing] this night forever?"

*

I frequently tell students to find a voice or form in which to write—a stylistic or rule-based mode, respectively, within which to "improvise." As a head suggests harmonic vocabulary, as a tempo and a time signature suggest rhythmic possibilities, so voice and form help writers, experienced and in-, see or hear or feel when their writing has derailed . . . or ought to.

*

Nobody quite "used" silence like Miles, whose solos often feel like erasures of previous solos. One can almost hear the notes between the notes.

*

When she accidentally skips a few lyrics in a children's song, my daughter will yell: "Papa! I missed a page! I missed a page, Papa!"

*

The jazz musicians with whom I used to play generally refused to talk about our music before we played, because it—the music—was its own conversation, and we didn't want our ordinary talk to prescribe or limit or confine in any way our musical "talk." Still, between sets, we often swapped stories about playing on the road, about our worst gigs, worst audiences, worst venues—I once played at the end of a long narrow vomit-reeking hallway, just outside the doors of a gilded theater ("success" dangling, so to speak, before my eyes), where a more popular group was set to play when we were finished—or else we shared anecdotes about famous jazz musicians. These stories not only deepened and made indelible the experience of playing, but also returned us to the stage reinvigorated, enriched: they unexpectedly colored or patinated our (or at least *my*) playing. And had the audience been privy to our extra-musical, betwixt-set convos, would it not have colored their listening, too?

*

Phillip Lopate's "Notes Toward an Introduction," which opens his 2003 essay collection, *Getting Personal: Selected Writings,* consists of five "unfinished" vignettes about some aspect of essay writing ("On the Confessional Mode," "On the 'I' Persona," "On Style," and so on), followed by an "Afterword" purportedly written by a Dr. Horst Shovel. "These scattered notes were found on the desk of my late friend," the doctor writes, "after his fatal aneurysm. They were meant to form the core of an introduction to his Selected Writings." What follows is a conversational evaluation of Lopate's oeuvre, alternately aggrandizing and deprecating. The kicker, the expectation-breaker, my perceptive students realize, is that Lopate is still alive, and Dr. Horst Shovel is in fact his invention.

Students think such a conceit requires a great deal of inventiveness, and maybe it does. But I like to believe that Lopate, no doubt a voracious reader, had chanced upon a similar approach to an introduction elsewhere. In "Unpacking My Library," Walter Benjamin discusses a rare, sought-after book called *Fragmente aus dem Nachlass eines jungen Physikers* [Posthumous Fragments of a Young Physicist]. "This work," writes Benjamin, "has never been reprinted, but I have always considered its preface, in which the author-editor tells the story of his life in the guise of an obituary for his supposedly deceased unnamed friend—with whom he is really identical—as the most important sample of personal prose of German Romanticism." Sometimes, I tell my students, creativity begins simply as imitation.

*

Balzac, on his deathbed, was said to have called out for a Dr. Bianchon: "Bianchon, the fictitious Bianchon, a doctor who existed only in the mind of Balzac" (Evan S. Connell).

*

Writing as a site for the expression of predetermined content perplexes me; the contents of my own work seem occultly awakened through language-play, which very often, even if the texts themselves are quite bad, surprise me. "Looking back on it," said E.M Forster of the artist at work, "he will wonder how on earth he did it. And indeed he did not do it on earth." However New Agey or sophomoric or naïve it may sound, I can't help but approach the blank page the way a jazz musician approaches a solo: I have nothing in mind—no agenda at all—except perhaps some self-imposed technical challenge (*I'll try the Egyptian scale on the turnaround*).

*

In William March's fable "The Young Poet and the Worm" (1940), an ethnocentric white male poet appraises both "this rich, perfect world which God created for man's pleasure!" and his own "plump, pink body." Whereupon a worm, down below, replies: "I don't know about that, but there's one thing I do know from my own experience: the perfection of man was assuredly made for the pleasure of worms."

*

The spirit or psychology of the jazz musician—in whose hands failure is inevitable, who is accepting of partial failure, who deems perfection a chimera, whose very art depends upon not looking back, upon concentrating wholly on the present and to hell with mistakes—has helped me laugh at overblown claims (Shelley: "Poets are the unacknowledged legislatures of the world"; Emerson: "[The poet] stands among partial men for the complete man, and apprises us not of his wealth, but of the commonwealth") about writing and the role of writers in the world.

*

The first books I fell in love with—Cormac McCarthy's early novels in particular—were ingested in great chunks of enthralled ignorance. I had no idea what was happening in these books, and I didn't care. I was simply smitten with—well, *the music of language.* I no longer find this an embarrassing admission, though I still occasionally feel a deep-seated insecurity. "Wait a second," I say to myself, dropping the book in my lap, "am I doing this right?"

*

Four years in a row, we were hired by a mortuary to play upbeat New Orleans-style jazz for All Souls' Day. One year, they had us set up in front of a small building out among the candlelit headstones. "This is an all-time low," our guitarist said, looking around. "Playing for dead people."

*

When I got off the phone with my father, who had called to tell me his own father, my grandfather, had died, I did not put on a record. I did not lift from its red case the old Hohner 64 chromatic harmonica that he gave me one year for Christmas. No. Instead I walked—floated?—to my bookshelf and pulled down Louise Glück's *A Village Life* (2009). I believed, in the soundless vertigo of grief, that one of these villagers' lost, elegiac voices was in fact the voice of my grandfather.

*

It's a cliché, but it's true: Writing, like most worthwhile undertakings, combats the finality of death.

*

Years ago, when Kali and I lived in San Francisco, we would occasionally stop at a small café on 9th and Irving, where a framed black-and-white photograph of Billie Holiday hung: the once-gorgeous singer standing before a studio vocal mic, haggard, unable (it appears) to lift her head, carrying in one hand a gin or vodka on the rocks. We are meant, I believe, to admire her in this photograph, as though the image contained the same strong fragility of her voice, or as though she was the Ancient Mariner—and she was not—even if her head hung as though an albatross weighed it down. Why else would the photograph be so elegantly framed? In truth, Holiday couldn't have been older than forty-four, and was no doubt suffering from cirrhosis of the liver, which is what would soon kill her.

*

and I am sweating a lot by now and thinking of
leaning on the john door in the 5 SPOT
while she whispered a song along the keyboard
to Mal Waldron and everyone and I stopped breathing

—Frank O'Hara, from "The Day Lady Died"

*

Geoff Dyer, from *But Beautiful: A Book About Jazz* (1996): "No other art form more ravenously investigates T.S. Eliot's famous distinction between that which is dead and that which is already living."

*

LIBERTY CITY
for Jaco Pastorius

July and the Hudson glittering and Jaco dives
right in, half naked, bronzed in sunlight,
to touch the Statue of Liberty.

I just stand there holding his Phillies cap.
"He should've died a long time ago," says a man
dressed like the ghost of Jimi Hendrix.

"A visitation," says Bill Milkowski, years later,
peering out the airplane window at Our Lady
Queen of Heaven and all the drifting clouds . . .

*

Miles did the music to Louis Malle's 1958 film *Ascenseur pour l'echafaud*. Though Miles and the four talented French musicians with whom he would play had seen the film and discussed ideas prior to recording the soundtrack, nothing had been written. There was no score. When it came time to record, Malle simply projected the film onto a screen and the musicians improvised to the images.

*

Shamala Gallagher: "We will make ourselves, in the image of our longing."

*

My first and only bass teacher, Mike Kelly, was blind. He taught me to listen first and understand later. And when I began to read and write, I once again listened first: I read an embarrassment of books, early in my literary life, without understanding them at all, though their semantic content, *their meaning*, cannot be extricated from their sound, their sonic persuasion, their style.

*

Music is often considered the most abstract of the arts, and it's difficult to disagree. For one, it's invisible (even if sound never ceases interacting with particles in space). Secondly, music cannot approximate language in the way that language can approximate music—it cannot, for example, invade the communicatory domain of language (give you directions, or teach you how to tie your shoes, even if a musician like Steve Vai can make his guitar "talk"). Nevertheless, for musicians, music is overwhelmingly tactile, and we also *see* the music in a variety of virtual forms: as notes on a staff, as a geometrical design on a fretboard, as notation on the Guidonian hand, as a series of numerical chords (e.g. I-vi-ii-V). As for the communicatory domain of language—and I'm speaking as a musician here—I feel that music communicates so much *in the language of music* that it almost warrants conventional linguistic communication null and void.

And yet here I am writing this . . .

*

One might reasonably assume that a jazz record is equivalent to a book. But this is not so. Almost all jazz records are nothing more than live performances captured in the studio; they are literally records of what was played on a particular day by a particular group of musicians—very much an anomaly nowadays. (Most records are made painstakingly piecemeal, each instrument replacing the original live track of itself, so that in the end the musicians have collaborated not with one another but with pasted-together recordings of one another.) Hence, a jazz record is nothing at all like a book, which arrives in our hands as a set-in-stone artifact, the singular goal and product of several years of composition. A book, even if it feels alive and in motion as we read it, exists in one and only one form.

*

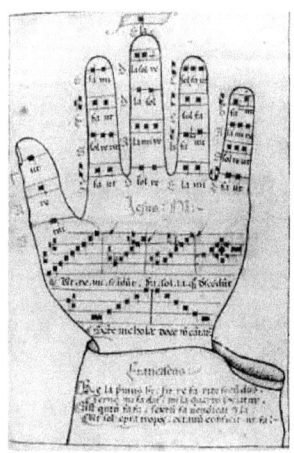

Can it be abstract?—
As Stravinsky said it must be to be music.
But what if a phrase could represent a thought—

—Donald Justice, from "The Sunset Maker"

*

This essay is being (so to speak) overdubbed, being made piecemeal: I write a number of "notes," then I go back and write notes between or around the notes, a kaleidoscope of notes, a constellation, an ornate arpeggio of notes, adding nuance and clarity and perhaps unnecessary apologias, technical digressions. Even so, the essay—the kind of writing and approach to composition I've been discussing—is still an attempt at jazzlike improvisation: I simply read something I've written, and then I write something "off" of it.

*

I do an exercise with students in which we all, myself included, write "versions" of a single sentence. Twenty-two versions of, for example, this sentence from Virginia Woolf's "Street Haunting": "The shell-like covering which our souls have excreted to house themselves, to make for themselves a shape distinct from others, is broken, and there is left of all these wrinkles and roughnesses a central oyster of perceptiveness, an enormous eye." Afterward, we split into groups and combine portions of our sentences into a single composite sentence. One rainy morning several weeks ago, a group produced this: "The yellow raincoats that our bodies have removed to make us look different again, inside this classroom, lay like shed second skins at our feet, and there is beneath each of these wet, wrinkled, glossy rubber jackets a little puddle of rainwater, the history of where we have been." Not bad for a twenty-minute exercise.

I find it fascinating, too, that they may have been unconsciously influenced by the sentence I'd given them a week earlier (from Baldwin's *Giovanni's Room*): "Every day the book-stall keepers seemed to have taken off another garment, so that the shape of their bodies appeared to be undergoing a most striking and continual metamorphosis."

*

Zeina Hashem Beck (from a personal interview): "One of the things I love most about listening to Arabic tarab music is the repetition of certain sentences and musical phrases over and over again until you feel you are almost drunk with them."

*

Allen Ginsberg once advised Robert Creeley to write in notebooks, as opposed to a typewriter, so he could be more mobile. Meanwhile, musicians all across the world are lugging drums and amps and double basses and PAs onto stages and up stairwells and in and out of the backs of vans — more mobile than any poet in history, possibly. For those of us who have been musicians, a typewriter doesn't seem so cumbersome at all. I much prefer Ginsberg's other advice regarding notebooks — that poets should frequently and experimentally alter the size of their notebooks, seeing as the length of a poem's lines is so often determined by the size of the notebook in which it was drafted.

*

I will sometimes write sentences as though I'm stepping on a piano's sustain pedal. Massive, many-handed sentences.

*

For many students, the five-paragraph essay or the three-quarter-page paragraph is a difficult convention to break. Furthermore, the allegiance to or the convenience of writing on a computer or typewriter (to say nothing of academic conventions/aesthetic vogues) creates rather arbitrary visual standards. How would your writing change if you had to write by hand on, say, an enormous art easel?

*

Jazz improvisation is not a deliberate manipulation of listeners' emotions, but rather a struggle (a positive word, in this case) among musicians to manipulate and be manipulated by one another. In jazz, the listener is a voyeur, not an addressee. I believe the same is true for a lot of writing—for a lot of my favorite writing, anyway: the reader does not *receive* a text, but is simply witness to an event in language; if in fact there is an addressee(s), then the reader overhears the address or pretends s/he is being addressed. Incidentally, this is perhaps why jazz and so-called "difficult" writing lack mass appeal and are, on the whole, commercial failures.

*

I played electric bass for the DeWald-Taylor Quintet for over a decade. We mostly played wineries, uppity "romantic" restaurants, political shindigs, and weddings. We were performing a service, and there were rules of etiquette, but we never let this stifle our creativity. As I often tell my students, you can write for a grade, you can perform a service, you can abide by academic (or any other) conventions, etc, but this doesn't mean you cannot be creative, too.

*

Most of us writers have no audience outside of (if we're lucky) our beloveds, our families, our close friends; and our texts are a means to communicate with them, directly or indirectly, about ourselves and about the world in our own, linguistically unique voices. Ergo: when Kali reads something I've written, I feel it has found its audience.

*

I once attended an Al Di Meola solo acoustic guitar concert at a winery outside Sacramento. Afterward, he shook hands and signed records. I handed him my copy of his first studio album, *Land of the Midnight Sun* (1976). At that time, I wore long hair and an impressive beard—a beard like the Miller in *The Canterbury Tales*: "fox-red and as broad as a shovel." Al asked me my name. "Jaydn," I told him. Then he began to write and speak at the same time. "To Lon Chaney . . ." he slowly intoned.

*

To make the experience of reading all the more intimate, one tends to read alone, in a semi-quiet place, holding the book, if one is like me, close to one's chest. Very different than encountering graffiti or a mass-produced pamphlet on a crowded street. And reading poetry is perhaps even more intimate, seeing as a poem tends to be fairly short, which means there's an attempt—isn't there?—to say more than its few words superficially express.

*

Jazz speaks to everybody. Writing speaks to everybody, too, but must be translated. Drop a Mumbai street musician into a New York club and s/he, who cannot speak a lick of English, will soon be soloing over rhythm changes.

*

Kali will sometimes look at my fingers on my thigh or on our steering wheel and, tilting her head, ask: "What are you playing?" I won't even realize, until that moment, that I had been playing anything.

*

Once, in high school, when playing in a rock band, our singer began to talk at length to the audience between tunes. I rudely cut him off by playing the well-known "Shave and a Haircut" (D-A-A-B-A), to which our guitarist, not missing a beat, responded: "Two bits" (C#-D).

*

When I watched *The Conversation* with my students this semester, for our obsession-themed first-year composition course, I realized I had to qualify my statements vis-à-vis privacy and writing. "Despite the privacy of composition," I told them, as the muted credits rolled on the projector screen and across—mockingly?—my face and body, "to ignore the overheardness of writing, to ignore the fact that somebody may read what you have written, that your work may indeed be 'bugged,' is to pretend that the world does not exist, and that you are not a part of it."

*

For several years in my late teens, I was in a rock band called Red Top Road—I won't comment on the quality of the music—playing the same few songs in pretty much the same way every night, which is to say our music was about as unsurprising as a recitation, though we did have an enjoyable "stage show": we jumped and wheeled and convulsed all over the stage. In fact, I think the majority of our fans just liked to see us go crazy. (Somewhere somebody has a video in which I'm hanging from the rafters of a low-ceilinged basement bar in downtown Sacramento called Scratch 8, my bass flung behind my back like an AK-47.) When we appeared on the cover of *Alive & Kicking*, a music-based Sacramento magazine, the large black-and-white photograph was of our singer, lead guitarist and me all in the air—a synchronized jump?—while under our legs was printed: "Sacto's Eight Legged Freaks."

Though our acrobatic performances were a far cry from a jazz concert, we were still deeply invested in providing a lot more than our records (we made three EPs on a now-defunct indie label) allowed, and seeing us one night might feel, even if we played the same songs, very different than the next. My extended interest and experience in performance has on the whole deflated my interest in the typical literary or academic reading, because a reading has never seemed to me an intrinsic element of writing itself, but rather an extracurricular social activity, even if it can be an enjoyable act of sharing, of community-building, of solidarity.

*

The best jazz musicians can play the same tune again and again, and each take will be significantly different. I've been playing a tune like "So What?" for almost twenty years. I'm well aware by now that if I grow bored with a tune, it's my fault: I didn't make it mine, or rather ours, and I didn't surprise myself, much less anybody else. Jazz is, as Whitney Balliett famously said, the sound of surprise.

*

When he asked the class to share our favorite music, I told my sixth-grade teacher, Mr. Taylor, that I liked jazz. He didn't believe me, so I told him I'd bring in Miles' *Kind of Blue*. The next day I handed him the cassette, he popped it in the boombox, and the music that issued forth for all my classmates genuinely mortifies me to this day: country music, Reba McEntire, one of my mother's tapes. *The sound of embarrassment.* Mr. Taylor guffawed, clapped his hands, bent over double, wheezed, had to catch his breath, so satisfied was he that I'd outed myself as a phony.

He was a musician, a guitarist. As though to finally prove to him the authenticity of my love for jazz, I would later play with him in a jazz combo for over a decade.

*

During my freshman year of high school, skater Jamie Thomas founded Zero, a now-legendary skateboard company. At the end of their debut video, *Thrill of It All*

(1997), Thomas performs what came to be known as the "Leap of Faith": he ollies over a second-story handrail, melon-grabs his board—that is, his forward (left) arm reaches behind and grabs the middle of the board—and then lands, solidly, snapping the board in two.

*

For about a year after the release of *Thrill of It All*, my friends and I skated nothing but stairs and gaps and sheer drops. If one of us was scared, if one of us stood at the edge of a grocery-store loading dock, for example, sheepishly tapping the tail of his board against the ground, then the others would begin to holler: "Leap of faith! Leap of faith!" This meant you had to do it—whatever it was you wanted to do.

*

My childhood home contained more fake books than actual books.

*

SET LISTS

1
Three o'clock in the Morning
Full Moon and Empty Arms
Strange Meadow Lark
Hawk Eyes
Black Orpheus
Mighty Lonesome Feeling

2
My Funny Valentine
Your Feet's Too Big (Guest Vocal)
So What
Take the "A" Train
Appointment in Ghana
I Surrender, Dear

3
In Walked Bud
Handful of Keys (Piano Feature)
Dizzy Atmosphere
Run the Voodoo Down
No Room for Squares
On Green Dolphin Street

4
Self-Portrait in Three Colors
Cherokee
Mr PC
Mysterious Traveler
Boulevard of Broken Dreams
It's Only a Paper Moon

*

Many years ago, on my father's backyard patio, my friend watched in astonishment as I invasively and adventurously edited Ernest Hemingway's *A Farewell to Arms* with a fine-point blue Sharpie. "Are you editing *Hemingway*?" he snapped.

I shrugged, capped the Sharpie, then continued reading. And for a long time afterward I felt unreasonably guilty—a child caught with his hand in the proverbial cookie jar.

I now do this very exercise with my students.

*

In Kihachiro Kawamoto's animated short *A Poet's Life* (1974)—based on a short story by Kobo Abe—a factory worker fired for demanding higher wages sends "words to shore up [other workers'] withering spirits." His mother, meanwhile, is inexplicably woven into a sweater and subsequently sold to a general store, where she lies folded and untouched in a dark storeroom. When a terrible winter befalls the town, and everybody freezes to death, a mouse in search of a warm nest wounds the sweater: "Accidentally, her teeth pierced the heart of the mother." The sweater bleeds, turns bright red—the only color in the film—and then soars like a ghost out of the store and through the lifeless, snow-covered town until she finds her son standing frozen in the street. She slips herself around his arms and torso, and he is revived. What's more, "[he] suddenly realized that he was a poet."

*

One of the first intertitles in *A Poet's Life* is a single Japanese character—"Mother."

*

In the sixth grade, I was chubbier and taller than most of my peers. My mother suggested I play the bass because, she said, I looked the part. One naturally (even if wrongly) associates a person's body with the sound of his or her music.

*

Saxophonist Anthony Braxton often uses little sketches—bizarre shapes, a set of data-like numbers ("W503")—as titles. He seems to be challenging the idea that a musical composition can be summed up in a single word or phrase (e.g. "Tenderly," "In a Sentimental Mood," "Bouncing with Bud"). Hearing this, one of my students erased the title of her essay about her mother's battle with breast cancer and replaced it with a sketch of a heart.

*

I often revolve my sentences around a word that has a particularly pleasant mouthfeel.

*

On summer days, when I can write at my dining room table from morning to late afternoon, I routinely walk (or am dragged by Kali or our kids) away with no more than a hard-won line or two. Then at night, slicing a peach or brewing a pot of decaf, I listen to Coltrane at Carnegie Hall soloing like a volcano gushing lava full blast. "Sheets of sound," critic Ira Gitler once described it.

*

O, how it deepens the night's color, / takes possession of the soundless air—

*

EVENING SKETCH: AFTER GOETHE

Quiet Over Calypso's island,	Quiet	Over all the hillsides.
Over all the mountains—	There is quiet.	Over all the treetops,
Can you hear,	In all her date palms,	In all the treetops,
In all the pine trees,	You can hear	Not even a hint
Even the tiniest breath,	Hardly a breath;	Of breath;
The sparrow asleep in her forest?	The starlings sleep in her forest.	Birds in the woods are silent.
Listen: in no time	Wait: sooner or later	Say, what do you say
You, too, will rest.	Even you must rest.	We, too, lie down and rest?

Over all her hillsides,	Over all the summits,	Over all our mountains,
Quiet. It is quiet;	There is quiet;	
In all her birch trees,	Over all the plane trees,	In all our treetops,
Not even a breath	Not even a breath	You can hear
Of leaves. Of wind.	Hardly a breath—	
Her birds in the woods are silent.	The owls in the woods are silent.	The birds have silenced our forest.
Wait: soon Listen: soon	Just wait: soon enough	
You, too, shall sleep.	You will be quiet too.	You (even you) will rest.

The Music Does Not Matter
NOTES ON MUSIC IN LITERATURE

> *You can put the listener in a room that doesn't exist, that couldn't exist. You can put them in an impossible room.*
> —Hari Kunzru

In Edward Bellamy's Marxist utopian novel *Looking Backward* (1888), Julian West—a late-nineteenth-century insomniac who, as a result of a particularly intense hypnosis-induced sleep, wakes up in the year 2000—is introduced to a "music room" ("an apartment finished, without hangings, in wood, with a floor of polished wood") and handed a card bearing "the longest program of music I had ever seen . . . a most extraordinary range of vocal and instrumental solos, duets, quartets, and various orchestral combinations." In Bellamy's imagined future, performance halls are connected by telephone wires to music rooms all across Boston, "'providing everybody with music in their homes, perfect in quality, unlimited in quantity, suited to every mood, and beginning and ceasing at will.'" Setting aside the omission of any non-classical musical genres, Bellamy is quite prescient: today, most of us possess mobile devices capable of accessing almost any music at almost any time, our own portable "music rooms." And yet, paradoxically, the music conjured in the music rooms of *Looking Backward*—like music in literature or, indeed, in any text at all—cannot be heard: it is soundless music, and thus exists solely in the imaginations of readers, an aural instantiation of what Bertrand Russell calls *sensibilia*—"unsensed sense-data."

Though he "remained bewildered by the prodigious list," Mr. West rather promptly chooses "an organ piece" and afterward exclaims that Bach himself "must be at the keys." So: *What have readers heard, exactly?* Some readers might "hear" something vaguely Bach-like—up-tempo contrapuntal organ perhaps? Others might not hear any music at all, but imagine a certain moment in German history, or an angelic church service, or an "important" bourgeois leisure pursuit, or— But the point is clear enough: the response music in literature triggers in a diverse audience is far from precise; hence, an unbridgeable gap separates those experiencing music in the domain of a literary work (such as Mr. West) from those reading about that music and/or the experience of it.

Counterintuitively, however, this "unbridgeable gap" has its advantages: for many writers, it creates among other things an extra-literary space in readers' minds, a tear in the fabric of the literary artifact/artifice, a mystery toward which we are perpetually drawn without the possibility of "answers"—a kind of Zeno's paradox. As Christopher Gilbert writes in "Listening to Monk's *Mysterioso*, I Remember Braiding My Sister's Hair":

> What it's all about is being
> just beyond a man's grasp
> which is a kind of consciousness
> you can own, to get to
> be at a moment's center
> and let it keep on happening
> knowing you don't own it—

For this reason, music in literature leads quite naturally to group formation and solidarity, as well as to transcendence—critic Stephen Benson refers to fictional transcendence through music as, simply, "the transcendence trope"—and corresponding forms of corporeal release/escape, the "rushing toward annihilation and embrace" (Rafi Zabor). In *Hoop Roots: Playground Basketball, Love, and Race* (2001), John Edgar Wideman writes, "*Transcendent* is a word that comes to mind when I consider the capacity of music to expand the parameters of experience upward, elevating the spirit, extending the range of what's possible. Music ushers in a transcendent reality."

Descriptions of Music in Literature

How, then, do poets and writers portray music in literature, seeing as it cannot be heard? Descriptions of music in literature tend to be sensuous, simile- and metaphor-laden evocations—Rachel Zucker: "'I sing like a rusty gate'"; Jackie Kay: "The sax was all slow and sad, like it was trying to remember something lost"; Reuben Jackson: "the music reveals itself / a negligee black note at a time"—which is just to make the obvious observation that the most common and effective descriptions of music tend to describe something other than music, even when descriptions of music are themselves "musical"—that is to say, when they aim to sonically imitate the music itself. "Zip little silver birds like buckshot dimes," writes Fred Chappell in his poem "The Highest Wind That Ever Blew: Homage for Louis." Or, "Ma's skirt balloons, his jacket booms. She zincs. He chowders," as Reginald McKnight writes in his short story "This Is How You Get to the 40s."

In contrast to, say, conventional notions/examples of *ekphrasis*, which attempt to inhabit and dramatize a still original, music in literature is generally twice removed: not only is music, *actual* music, rather than the proverbial "music of poetry" or the musical form of a novel such as Toni Morrison's *Jazz*, incapable of existing in literature, but the descriptions that stand in for music (Bernard Malamud: "The song was like a lit candle in the night") almost always refer to nonmusical sensuous particulars, commonly through similes and metaphors, so that the effect is less palimpsestic than it is intersemiotic: it is music translated or transcribed into sensuous verbal descriptions, and the music on the page—if one persists in thinking of it as music proper—is a fantasy impossible to actualize, an art forever poised on the edge of being. This is "the bind in which the musically-interested writer finds her or himself," observes Stephen Benson in *Literary Music: Writing Music in Contemporary Fiction* (2006), "—music is interesting for its musicality, but it is this above all else that will escape the writing." In lieu of music, then, we have writerly flourishes, attempts to compensate in other ways for literature's inability to (re)produce actual music.

An ekphrastic description, however imaginative or whimsical or animated it may be, must maintain an imagistic relationship to the image it is meant to describe or affectively augment. Descriptions of music are not bound to the image of a band performing, or a neighbor practicing her *lieder* (to evoke Ralph Ellison's "Living with Music"), or speakers stationed in two corners of a room. Rather, descriptions of music are bound to the "original" auditory phenomena issuing from those images. The writer or narrator or speaker is free, or at least *freer* than the ekphrastic writer-narrator-speaker, to go beyond conventional sensory descriptions, to translate intersemiotically, to introduce that which is seemingly unrelated to the "original" music, even as it describes and augments it.

But why not, one might ask, *a technical description of music?* Setting aside the obvious fact that, to a nonmusician readership, a technical description of music will be incomprehensible (Vikram Seth: "a rapid figure in pizzicato quartertones"), many writers themselves do not possess a clear understanding of either music theory or instrumental technique. There are, of course, notable exceptions: David Shapiro was a violin prodigy; Nicholson Baker was briefly a bassoonist for a philharmonic orchestra; and Reuben Jackson was for many years curator of the Duke Ellington Collection at the Smithsonian in Washington, D.C. In any case, for the music-invested writer, to misdescribe or explain incorrectly some technical aspect of music is to risk discrediting whatever authority s/he may have previously held.

Frank Conroy, who writes about music exquisitely in his memoirs *Stop-Time* (1967) and *Time & Tide: A Walk through Nantucket* (2004), and especially in his first and only novel *Body & Soul* (1993), nevertheless describes at length, in an essay called "Think About It," his own misunderstanding of what pianist Red Garland was "doing with his left hand." Conroy writes, "I went uptown to an obscure club where [Red] was playing with his trio, caught him on his break, and simply asked him. 'Sixths,' he said cheerfully. And then he went away." Years later, Conroy "discovers" that "if the bass played the root [of a dominant-seventh chord] and I played the sixth based on the fifth note of the scale, an interesting chord involving both instruments emerged." That "interesting chord" is simply a major third. If the root is a C, then six of five (G) is an E. (Isn't it more interesting if he played the key's actual sixth [A], with the dissonance it creates beside the dominant seventh [B-flat]?) Far more egregious than Conroy's misunderstood "epiphany" surrounding Garland's one-word explanation ("Sixths") is his insistence that, after many years of living with it, "my life caught up with the information and the lightbulb went on." Musician-readers do not experience the illumination Conroy had intended—instead, they are still waiting for him to be illuminated rightly—and nonmusician-readers may have glossed over the passage altogether, lost at sea.

My point here is not to shame Conroy—"Think About It" is a fine essay, and it's not fundamentally about music, anyway—or criticize musicality in toto. (Check out these lines, from Marvin Bell's "The Fifties," which offer something for musicians and nonmusicians alike: "I see notes for solos—bad. / I get hung on the chords—bad. / I can't stay up—bad"). My point here is to display how distant technical descriptions of music remain from actual experiences of music. However unintuitive it may be, those "sensuous, simile- and metaphor-laden evocations" discussed above far better approximate our experiences of music, despite their turning away from music itself. It turns out that "this fearful medium," as Tolstoy writes in *The Kreutzer Sonata*, "is available to anyone who cares to make use of it."

Abstract / Invisible Realities: Integration, Transcendence, Escape

In "The Hallelujah Chorus," according to Ed Pavlić's *Who Can Afford to Improvise?: James Baldwin and Black Music, the Lyric and the Listeners* (2016), Baldwin tells Ray Charles that music is "an abstract reality." This is undoubtedly true. It's one of the reasons why the Abstract Expressionists—thanks in part to Clement Greenberg's "Towards a Newer Laocoön": "[I]n its nature [music] is the art furthest removed from imitation"— so admired music. Yet music is also an *invisible reality*: we can watch musicians perform or turntables spin, but we cannot watch music (or any auditory phenomena) itself. Sound is "suspended in the air, detached from the solidity of things," to quote Italo Calvino's "A King Listens."

As a result, sound's invisibility, in tandem with the soundlessness of literature, facilitates the bending of reality in literature, however slight. In David Huddle's novella *Tenorman* (1995), Eddie Carnes' seductive tenor playing— playing that "could unhook a bra"—is seductively directed at female listeners: "'As a woman, you sense that you're the *object* of that music,'" says Marianne, the narrator's wife. In Josef Škvorecký's short story "Eine Kleine Jazzmusik," a trumpet player can "attack" a Nazi with his horn: "In a unisono blast the brass gave forth a fortissimo bellow as if straight at his person. Everything went black before his eyes . . ." This invisible, soundless "music" also allows Emma's resonating piano to be heard across an entire village in this well-known passage from *Madame Bovary* (trans. Lydia Davis):

> She would strike the keys with assurance and run down the entire keyboard from top to bottom without stopping. When it was thus assaulted by her, the old instrument, with its buzzing strings, could be heard as far as the edge of the village if the window was open, and often the bailiff's clerk, who was passing on the main road, bareheaded and in slippers, would stop to listen, holding his piece of paper in his hand.

Like long-lost family members, like unexpected weather, like phone calls in the middle of the night, music can suddenly arrive, bearing its associations and moods, its emotional capabilities and anonymous unseen performer(s). In "The Singing Simics," Charles Simic describes his uncle Boris singing opera on a New York subway: "I recall the astonished faces of sleepy passengers . . . opening their eyes wide to find in their midst Andrea Chénier himself, the great French Romantic poet and innocent victim of revolutionary justice dying on the guillotine and singing with his last breath." And, similarly, in Wanda Coleman's "Jazz at Twelve," the narrator can hear, upon seeing her boyfriend's "moonful look, the one that tells me I'm beautiful. . . . Nat King Cole singing 'Angel Eyes.'" The invisible reality of music draws music-in-literature into the domain of the imagination—even if, as Benson observes, "music is always already worldly: socially situated, entwined with words, however silently."

It should come as no surprise, then, that music in literature is capable of doing more in the world of the relevant text than music is capable of doing in the world itself. (Like the Afrohorn in Henry Dumas's "Will the Circle Be Unbroken?" which can kill "uninitiated" listeners, e.g. white listeners, listeners for whom its rare and ancient music is not intended.) Nor should it come as a surprise that this essay opened with a passage from a utopian novel: it's crucial to foreground the illimitableness of music in literature—the very ease with which it transcends the bounds of reality.

> The music Pythagorean,
>   one note at a time
> Connecting the heavenly spheres. (Simic)

In Kazuo Ishiguro's phantasmagoric novel *The Unconsoled* (1995), music is a liberating force, a force capable of rousing a city: Ryder, widely regarded as the greatest living pianist, is scheduled to give a concert, and the success of his performance—his ability to re-inspire them, or transport down to earth some fragment from the ineffable—is tied to the future of this unnamed Central European city. In *The Unconsoled*, writes Benson, "[m]usic is put to work in an essentially commodified fashion, as art with a use-value, that of consolation and reparation"—a use-value effortlessly upheld in literature, seeing as music (consigned therein to silence) is so frequently imbued with abstract potentiality, with the Platonic ideal of music. "And my ears *made* the blowing hymns they heard," writes Wallace Stevens in "Tea at the Palaz of Hoon" (my emphasis). Too, Ryder is a concert pianist, rather than a composer or improviser, and though interpretations of written music by musicians vary widely, not even Glenn Gould could make Bach sound unlike Bach: it's a translational skill, not a compositional one. Thus, in *The Unconsoled*,

Ryder's task—the performative expectations leveled upon him by a vast array of characters, known or unknown or once known (Ryder's former life with this city's populace dreamily and only fragmentarily surfaces: he has an ex-wife, a son, numerous "friends")—is even more outrageous: he must reinvigorate *known* commodities, make compositions already heard or at least capable of being heard, uplift an entire city.

Which is just to say that *The Unconsoled* exaggerates music's ability to unite people, provide a so-called "universal language," be an agent of group formation and solidarity. This is another trope of music-invested literature. The Trumpets of Zion form the social nucleus of James Baldwin's *Just Above My Head* (1979). Kanye's album *My Beautiful Dark Twisted Fantasy* is an invisible thread enwrapping isolated listeners in Kiese Laymon's "Kanye West and HaLester Myers Are Better at Their Jobs . . ." Music, too, is what keeps brothers Jonah and Joseph together in Richard Powers' *The Time of Our Singing* (2003), even if, finally, to quote A. Elizabeth Reichel, "it is social and political forces that decide whether music is able to create permanent alliances."

In Škvorecký's "Eine Kleine Jazzmusik," like *The Unconsoled* in its exaggeration of this trope, a jazz band known as the Masked Rhythm Bandits give a rapturous, climactic performance ("God Almighty, who has created jazz and all the beauties of the world, only you know how well we played!") in a Nazi-occupied Eastern European city referred to as K. The bandmembers are "masked" to preserve their identity. The familiar elements of jazz (swing, syncopation, scatting, etc) are effectively outlawed. In this scene, the Masked Rhythm Bandits' concert produces among its musicians as well as its audience—"a local *Wermacht* unit"—an extraordinary if short-lived freedom: "It seemed to me that the theatre in K. had disappeared . . . and there was nothing but music." By entering so completely the space in which music and music-listening occurs, almost every character present at that final concert in "Eine Kleine Jazzmusik" receives—semi-equally—a cathartic release from authoritarian decrees *and* a balm for whatever physical or psychic suffering has been and/or will be inflicted by them (*Wermacht*) or upon them (Masked Rhythm Bandits).

A brief transcendence, yes?

Because it cannot issue from the text itself, music in literature is often linked to life-altering experiences or momentous revelations: writers cannot help but explore the "wonder-working fantasy" (Hawthorne's phrase) of music. "Raise me up into that music by which all things are changed," writes Rafi Zabor. Of course, there's no shortage of historical musicians who believed some form of transcendence via music was possible—famously John Coltrane, whose late, avant-garde concerts and albums (see *Ascension*) were feverishly otherworldly—or else whose compositions attempted to transcend or at least transport its listeners (see Gustav Holst's *The Planets*). But such musicians and compositions are rare.

Meanwhile, literature routinely uses the present-absence of music, as well as the oft-startling descriptions that supplant music (Bob Kaufman: "Smothered rage covering pyramids of notes spontaneously exploding") to exploit the absorbing, transportive possibilities and emotional flights inherent to music. As John Edgar Wideman writes in his short story

"Williamsburg Bridge," "[O]ne afternoon Sonny Rollins practicing changes on the Williamsburg Bridge halts me dead in my tracks. Big colors, radiant bucketfuls splash my face. I spin, swim in colors. Enraptured. Abducted by angels who lift me by my droopy wings up, up, and away." Put differently, music in literature often disguises its inexpressibility as *ineffability*, producing an aesthetic and existential trapdoor—a tear in the fabric of the relevant literary artifact/artifice— through which readers, along with speakers or narrators or characters, enter (without entering) a realm beyond the limits of language. The Coltranian solo at the end of Rafi Zabor's *The Bear Comes Home* (1997) is the finest example I've yet encountered, hands down:

> . . . and the rush of his own ideas blasting him into regions unforeseen. He saw the treasured geometry of his lights and vitals, the wellscanned signature of his timeless self erased by waves of greater light, the vessel bursting, and as the Bear sped to the limits of his own transcendent outline, he could discern details—gardens, geometries, geometric gardens, fine dust and starry singularities, all the declensions of Life into lives—rushing toward annihilation and embrace, their mayfly construction swept away, since under these circumstances even metaphysical flesh was grass.
>
> He felt the the [sic] wellknown fluttering veil at the entrance of his heart give way as a greater paw lifted it like a piece of pop-up tissue paper.
>
> I don't believe this is ha—
>
> The whole world vanished. In fact all worlds vanished.

." . . and there was nothing but music," indeed.

Yet not all transportive/transcendent experiences of music in literature are otherworldly; some are afterworldly. In Jackie Kay's debut novel *Trumpet* (1998) —in a chapter simply titled "Music"—the spirit or soul or ghost of Joss Moody, legendary trumpet player and transgender man, escapes his body-vessel while playing music for the other bodies in the funeral parlor, "his stiff comrades inside their coffins." It's a long, feverish, metamorphic solo—in the course of which he witnesses his own birth, becomes a horse, becomes a girl again—"He can taste himself transforming"—and at last merges with music itself: "He *is* the music" (my emphasis). I say "becomes a girl again" not because Joss ever identified as female—definitely not—but because the metamorphic solo enables him to appear elsewhere in *Trumpet* in a variety of outward forms: "He is a girl. A man. Everything, nothing. He is sickness, health. The sun. The moon. Black, white." And most prominently, in the dreams of first Millie and then Colman, Joss appears in the form of "a small black girl"; "a small girl, his father." In any event, the chapter's indispensable, the principle moment in which Kay acknowledges her ethical bind: the potential harm of speaking of and about a transgendered man on the one hand (like the absence of Emmett Till's voice/perspective in Lewis Nordan's *Wolf Whistle*), and the ethnocentric artistic hubris of speaking as or for him (à la William Styron's *The Confessions of Nat Turner*) on the other. Insufficient to her art's demands, Kay exploits the present-absence of music in literature by allowing Joss to "speak" for himself (albeit inaudibly and incorporeally) as music, and thus become, in Wallace Stevens' familiar words, the "[n]othing that is not there and the nothing that is." Joss and music, now one and the same, there after haunt the novel like a ghost, like Scotland's atmospheric fog ("The people and the weather shrouded in uncertainty"), like the silent white space of a page.

On the Musical Imaginary

Now let us return more directly to the paradox of music in literature: how it provokes our listening but denies us music. It strikes me as too simple and dismissive to cast this paradox in a tragic light—"'That's the worst of music—these silly dreams!'" as a character exclaims in Virginia Woolf's "The String Quartet"—or to claim that readers are like Odysseus's shipmates, their ears plugged with beeswax, deaf to the Sirens' "high, thrilling song." After all, even if you cannot, like Odysseus, "hear the Sirens' song to your heart's content," music in literature can still access or activate the space in which music-listening occurs, an imaginary, unlocatable space—"the part of you projected into the space of sounds" (Calvino).

Consider the moment, in David Huddle's *Tenorman*, when Marianne describes her husband thus: "'I'd been standing there beside you—and I knew you'd "lifted off" the way you do when one of your old jazz guys picks up a horn and starts to play. You were up there in the zone.'" Or that moment when Millie—to return to Jackie Kay's *Trumpet*—at a jazz club with Joss, her soon-to-be husband, finds herself "inside the music": "I am sitting in the middle of the long slow moan of the sax, right inside it." In "Listening with Imagination: Is Music Representational?" philosopher Kendall Walton echoes this very sentiment: "it is as though I am inside the music, or it is inside me." Music in literature, as a record of music's existence, as an intersemiotic translation of music, opens both the desire and the eagerness to absorb music (or be absorbed by it), and this desire, this eagerness, becomes in turn a palpable, extra-literary presence—a present absence—that invisibly surrounds and soundlessly accompanies one's experience of reading. The activation of the music-listening process, even in the absence of actual music, becomes an ingredient of reading itself. Walton again: "It is as though the music provides the smile without the cat—a smile for the listener to wear." Put too succinctly, the paradox of music in literature enlarges readers' aesthetic, affective, and sensorial experience. There's no tragedy to the paradox because—to corrupt Eliot's infamous line of metacommentary ("The poetry does not matter") from *Four Quartets*—the *music* does not matter. What matters is the *musical imaginary*, the felt space readers enter as virtual listeners of a soundless music. (This, incidentally, is the chief reason I have employed the phrase "music in literature," as opposed to Stephen Benson's "literary music." I'm sympathetic to "literary music": music in literature is not, in truth, actual music, hence it requires the adverbial qualifier. Yet I prefer "music in literature" because there is, as I argue above, a constitutive element of music—the imaginary, unlocatable space of listening—present in reading of and about music.) "We might have known it always," writes David Malouf, "music / is the landscape we move through in our dreams."

ENVY OF OTHER PEOPLE'S POEMS

>In one version of the legend the sirens couldn't sing.
>It was only a sailor's story that they could.
>So Odysseus, lashed to the mast, was harrowed
>By a music that he didn't hear—plungings of sea,
>Wind-sheer, the off-shore hunger of the birds—
>
>And the mute women gathering kelp for garden mulch,
>Seeing him strain against the cordage, seeing
>The awful longing in his eyes, are changed forever
>On their rocky waste of island by their imagination
>Of his imagination of the song they didn't sing.
>
>—Robert Hass

Paralleling the inaudibility of music in literature, some of the most fascinating migrations into the musical imaginary are concerned with responses to music by somebody other than—but intimately related to—a speaker, narrator, or third-person protagonist. A key factor in the emotional impact of James Joyce's "The Dead," for example, lies in the disparity between Gabriel's response to his wife, Gretta, "standing on the stairs in the shadow, listening to distant music"—"A sudden tide of joy went leaping out of his heart"—and Gretta's own response to the music. Specifically, she remembers Michael Furey, who in her adolescence "used to sing that song, *The Lass of Aughrim*" and who, she believes, had died for her (aged seventeen) by visiting her, despite an illness, one cold dark wet night: "[I] slipped out the back into the garden and there was the poor fellow at the end of the garden, shivering."

Readers need not "hear" *The Lass of Aughrim* in some evocative verbal metaphor. After all, the version Gabriel all but distantly hears is supplanted by the image of his wife shadowed on the stairs—"*Distant Music* he would call the picture if he were a painter"—and the version Gretta hears is uniquely tied to her own experience, to which readers have, until she reveals the memory to Gabriel, no access at all. "Music is feeling, then, not sound," writes Wallace Stevens in "Peter Quince at the Clavier,"

> And thus it is that what I feel,
> Here in this room, desiring you,
> Thinking of your blue-shadowed silk,
> Is music.

And here, in Joyce's "The Dead," music is two distinct feelings, and thus separates man and wife. Contrary to music's integrative function—its ability to unite people far and wide: "Then suddenly, like a rope cast for rescue, the drums spanned the distance, gathering them all up and connecting them" (Toni Morrison)—Gabriel and Gretta hear different songs, cannot *not* hear different songs. (As an aside, viewers not need truly hear *The Lass of Aughrim,* anyway, at least the version Joyce intended. In "'Thought-Tormented Music': Joyce and the Music of the Irish Revival," Martin Dowling explains that the melody featured in John Huston's *The Dead* is "the Scottish, not the Irish, version.") Because the song on which this story turns is, for readers, inaudible—"distant music" indeed—the story dramatizes the musical imaginary: the music we "hear" or are prepared to hear exaggerates the idiosyncrasies inherent to music-listening and is capable of distancing, isolating even, one listener from another.

The migration into the musical imaginary is similarly dramatized in Ishiguro's "Crooner," from *Nocturnes: Five Stories of Music and Nightfall* (2009). Tony Gardner, a bygone American crooner gearing up for a "comeback," invites the narrator, a "gypsy" guitarist named Janeck, to accompany him during a private performance: Gardner wants to serenade his wife, Lindy, from a gondola—the story's set in Venice—beneath her balcony. However, when the gondola arrives at Lindy's window, a brief squabble about where Gardner has been ensues, and then Lindy complains of the cold, so that Gardner tells her to "listen from inside the room. . . . Just leave those windows open and you'll hear us fine." Ishiguro withholds the songs' lyrics, and the music itself is only cursorily described: "I tried to make it sound like America, sad roadside bars, big long highways"; or, "his voice came out just the way I remembered it—gentle, almost husky, but with a huge amount of body, like it was coming through an invisible mike." Finally, several tunes into their performance, Gardner and Janeck hear Lindy "up there sobbing." *Why? Is she sad, disappointed, overjoyed?* As Janeck himself asks Gardner: "'Just now, was Mrs. Gardner crying because she was happy or because she was upset?'"

Deaf to the intratextual music, readers can only guess at what the music might sound like and what, more importantly, it might mean to its addressee: Lindy's response to the music, to her husband's grandiloquent if stereotypical romantic gesture, cannot be parsed with any accuracy. (Thought experiment: *What if we could actually hear Gardner's serenade—if this were a film, say, and Gardner sang Frank Sinatra's "Moonlight Serenade"—would we ourselves project feelings of romance and hope onto Lindy's response?* It's not unlikely.) Because a detailed description of the serenade would in all likelihood clarify for reader-listeners how Lindy feels or, more precisely, how readers *think* she feels, Ishiguro chooses to let Lindy's response—as well as Janeck's response *to* her response: "'We did it, Mr. Gardner!' . . . 'We did it. We got her by the heart'"—create narrative tension, a mystery requiring clarity.

And Gardner soon clarifies: he tells Janeck that, although they've been married for twenty-seven years and are happy together, he and Lindy are divorcing. In the quasi-realism of *Nocturnes*, a crooner's "comeback" requires a young wife: "'Look at the ones from my generation still hanging round,'" Gardner tells Janeck. "'Every single one of them, they've remarried. Twice, sometimes three times. Every one of them, young wives on their arms. Me and Lindy are getting to be a laughing stock.'" The pathos of Ishiguro's "Crooner" is that the authenticity and the uses, or use-value, of the "love song"—the musical imaginary reader-listeners associate, say, with the Great American Songbook or the romance of Venice—are sacrificed on the altar of superficial American careerist ambitions.

Sound v. Image (Reprise)

Musical strains, well rendered, had a way of evoking pictures in her mind.

—Kate Chopin

Though it's an abstract *and* an invisible reality, by collaborating with the writer, with experience, with character, narrative, plot, setting, image, language—all those familiar characteristics of creative writing—music in literature nevertheless acquires (by proximity or osmosis) pictorial representation. "Music," according to Kendall Walton, "stands ready to take on an explicit representational function at the slightest provocation." A glaring example occurs in a late chapter of Jackie Kay's *Trumpet*, when Colman, Joss Moody's adopted son, remembers his father telling stories with his horn:

> As a treat sometimes, he would ask for ingredients to his story. Everyone present had to give one. Whatever you could think up. A butterfly. A chest. A little girl looking through a keyhole. Hair. A baby ape. An old woman in a house by the sea. And then he would make up a song on his trumpet, a song that would tell the story of all these things together, and sometimes it was possible for each person to recognize the music of the butterfly, of the wooden house, of the little girl.

Unlike Rimsky-Korsakov's "Flight of the Bumblebee," Maria Schneider's *Cerulean Skies*, or Mussorgsky's *Pictures at an Exhibition*—compositions that cannot *not* describe or collaborate with their titles—Joss's "story time" is a veritable flipbook of complex, emotionally suggestive images: "A butterfly" (whimsical?); "A chest" (nostalgia?); "A little girl looking through a keyhole" (fear? curiosity?); "Hair" (erotic?); "A baby ape" (cute?); "An old woman in a house by the sea" (lonesome?). Audible only in readers' imaginations, Joss's trumpet playing acquires the narratological abilities associated with literature and the paradigmatic representational arts—it narrativizes and brings to life, brings together, each person's "ingredient." It's a clever move. If Kay can convert music into evocative verbal descriptions, then she can "record" (for both her characters and her readers) Joss's music *without sound*.

There are countless, subtler examples of music in literature acquiring narratological meaning without sensuous, simile- or metaphor-laden descriptions. In Ed Pavlić's *Winners Have Yet to Be Announced* (2008), a copy of George Oppen's *Of Being Numerous* is slipped in the cover of a book on suicide and then placed on Donny Hathaway's piano "just to make people listen a little different"—or to make readers "listen" *a lot* different. Still, on the whole, such acquisitions occur most frequently when music becomes for its listener (narrator, speaker, character) the proverbial Proustian madeleine—a rabbit-hole into the past.

In James Alan McPherson's "Why I Like Country Music," from his 1977 Pulitzer prize-winning short story collection *Elbow Room*, a nameless African American narrator attempts to explain to his wife and to himself—indeed, "quietly, and mostly to myself"—the very task the title sets in motion. Put simply, the explanation is that country music, particularly when accompanied by square dancing, reminds him of his boyhood infatuation with a girl named Gwyneth Lawson, with whom he'd square-danced at a school performance. Country music plays throughout the two kids' climactic dance—." . . *promenade that dear old thing / Throw your head right back and sing* be-*cause, just* be-*cause* . . ."—but the sound of the music is not described. Instead, the music is supplanted by memories, those indelible images McPherson's retrospective narrator still fondly recalls: "I only remember that during many turns and do-si-dos I found myself looking into the warm brown eyes of Gwyneth Lawson. I recall that she smiled at me. I recall that she laughed on another turn. I recall that I laughed with her an eternity later." This sort of "recall" is a widespread literary tactic. "*Memoria* was [once] the mother of the muses," writes Victor Villanueva, "the most important of the rhetorical offices." Still, its execution—how one tackles such "personal, private, vanishing evocations," to corrupt a phrase from James Baldwin's "Sonny's Blues"—is varied and difficult, maybe even impossible. As McPherson's narrator later admits: "[A]lthough it is difficult to explain to you, I still maintain that I am no mere arithmetician in the art of the square dance. I am into the calculus of it." Though she may not be able to grasp "the calculus of it," the narrator's wife, like readers themselves, can certainly feel a more-than-modest portion of the lived experience embedded, for him, in country music.

This tactic can be turned on its head, too. Consider Ellen Douglas's *A Lifetime Burning* (1982), an inventive exploration of the confrontation between imagination and reality. An epistolary novel, *A Lifetime Burning* consists of the compelling, often scandalous "confessions"—that is to say, *lies*: "My dreams of my own frustration, impotence, passivity, hatred, imprisonment, death"—of a sixty-two-year-old wife, mother, and professor of literature named Corinne, as she angularly stumbles her way toward what she has been "putting off" for much of her adult life: her love affair with a woman named Judith. The novel seems to embrace D.H. Lawrence's claim that "out of a pattern of lies art weaves the truth." Like McPherson's "Why I Like Country Music," this text is addressed to Corinne's husband, George, as well as to her children, though it, too, is addressed quietly, and mostly to herself.

One of Corinne's wilder "confessions" concerns her month-long "sabbatical" in California: she stays with her son William, a singer-songwriter, and there befriends a rather unstable young woman named Janice Clifford, a viola player who rents a room in his house and is obsessed with American violinist Eugene Fodor. More specifically, after hearing/seeing Fodor on the Johnny Carson show—and Fodor was in fact a frequent guest on the show—Janice believes that she, and she alone in all the world, can sufficiently nurture a musician of such extraordinary talent and depth: "'[W]hen [Johnny] asked Eugene a question,'" she tells Corinne one afternoon, "'I saw an expression cross his face—Eugene's—indescribable, as if he retreated into some deep place inside himself. I knew and he knew—he would know, if only he had a chance to—that I was the only one who belonged there.'" Unlike McPherson's narrator, who attempts with appreciable success to communicate the relationship between country music and his first infatuation, Janice has no tangible relationship with Fodor, the man or the music: she is a mere listener-spectator, and whatever she hears when she hears him play has no basis in reality. When she states elsewhere that Fodor is a "prisoner of his gift," readers no doubt detect that Janice, alas, is the prisoner of her obsession. In this soft-edged California "sabbatical" at the center of *A Lifetime Burning*, music and musicians emerge as figures for the imagination itself, for the virtual and untenable realities that both Janice and Corinne have created—each in her own way—for themselves.

By this point in the novel, music and Corrine's imagination/lies have long been linked. In her first major invention, for example, she follows George into a church, attempting to catch him and their diminutive neighbor who she's cruelly nicknamed "The Toad" ("she has the look of someone who barely missed being a midget—arms a trifle short, a short-legged waddle for a walk") fornicating. In due course, Corinne hides in a dark, cramped closet—a not-so-subtle metaphor for the openness of her own sexuality—that opens into two rooms. In one room, she hears George and The Toad whisper-talking; in the other, the church choir and a pianist rehearsing. Naturally, the music cannot *not* comment upon or ornament Corinne's situation: when the pianist begins "Draw me nearer, nearer, nearer, blessed Lord," readers instinctively put this song title in different characters' mouths. *Is this what The Toad says, in so many words, to George? Is this what Corinne says/sings to herself as she overhears her husband cheating?* Several diary entries later, however, when we learn that Corinne has in fact invented the entire scene and that even The Toad is a fabrication, readers cannot help but mull over the title yet again. *Is this what Corinne says/sings as she imagines herself nearer, nearer, nearer to the truth?* Hence, what was at first commentary on Corrine's situation (i.e. her story) has now become metacommentary on her storytelling. When the choir sings "'Just as I a-am, Thy love I own . . .,'" Corrine remarks, "Ugh. Flat," whereupon she quits the closet and then the church, as though the remark ("Ugh. Flat") were leveled at her own powers of imagination, her own "[p]itiful sad illusions." Put simply, in Corrine's invented scene, the very mention of music creates a metafictive (non)space—another virtual and untenable reality—another impossible room— between the story and her ability to tell it.

But let us return to *sound* and *image*. Again, one might ask if there is a difference between sound and image in, frankly, any of the texts heretofore discussed. More precisely: *Is the kind of sight employed in looking at visual art also accessed and thenceforth carried about, so to speak, as a present absence throughout one's reading experience?* Yep, I think it is. In literature, however, auditory phenomena—to say nothing of music— are almost never "composed." (The "Sounds" chapter of Thoreau's *Walden* has its moments, and Italo Calvino's short story "A King Listens" is something of an anomaly: "For you the days are a succession of sounds, some distinct, some almost imperceptible; you have learned to distinguish them, to evaluate their provenance and their distance; you know their order, you know how long the pauses last; you are already awaiting every resonance or creak or clink that is about to reach your tympanum. . .") The composition of sound is most frequently employed for dramatic or suspenseful effect—like the ticking clock/heart in Edgar Allan Poe's "The Tell-Tale Heart." Unless one is John Cage, who listened to *everything* in the same way he listened to music, the auditory phenomena that accompany quotidian activity in literature and in life (footfalls on pavement, a cough behind a door do not access or activate the musical imaginary.

And yet it's quite commonplace to encounter, in literature, a painterly or filmic composition of characters and/or objects: "The two women are sitting at right angles to each other in the kitchen on a sunny July morning in the nineteen-sixties," begins Ellen Douglas' 1988 novel *Can't Quit You, Baby*. Moreover, there's no shortage of lyric poems that funnel down to a single, memorable, even haunting image:

> Light from the open car
> reveals the yard.
> And, as if painted onto the night,
> is the yellow window
> where someone, holding a mirror,
> is drawing a picture of herself. (Ondaatje)

Ergo, it's difficult for readers to extricate imagery from the kind of sight accessed when looking at visual art ("*ut pictura poesis*" — "as is painting so is poetry" — as Horace so famously put it), whereas it's very difficult indeed for readers to even associate auditory phenomena with the kind of hearing one accesses/activates when listening to music. Sound does not dominate in the way that imagery clearly does; thus, readers are far more likely to acutely register their migration into a musical imaginary than into a visual (art) imaginary.

Across or Among People: Baldwin and Authorial Intrusion

But of course literature cannot, like Corinne in California, like the prince in Poe's "The Red Masque of Death," sequester music into "castellated abbeys" of the imagination, in effect saying (to quote Poe's narrative): "The external world could take care of itself." Will not the Red Death visit us anon? To my mind, death will at least—or perhaps should I say "at last"—visit the work that abstains from communicating with a living, extratextual world. Langston Hughes: "Music . . . demanded movement and expression, dancing and living to go with it." Music in literature does not exist merely to activate an ideal music in readers' minds, but rather to record or to enact in language the effects of music across or among people, individually and collectively. Despite the prevalence of the transportive descriptions discussed above, music in literature is inextricably linked to language, characters, plot, settings, moods, form, historical period(s), and so on and so forth, in much the same way that music is inextricably linked to real people and places and emotional states and situations. Music, and music in literature, is a communal art. As Ondaatje writes of Fats Waller in his poem "In a Yellow Room," "I have always loved him but I love him most in the company of friends." Similarly, about Billie Holiday in "The Day Lady Died," Frank O'Hara writes, "she whispered a song along the keyboard / to Mal Waldron and everyone and I stopped breathing," so that we all—hearing about her death and, at the same time, "hearing" her whisper a song along a keyboard—stop breathing, *together*.

Furthermore, to borrow terminology from film, there is in literature no such thing as *non-diegetic* or *extradiegetic* sound: a reader cannot "hear" music that a narrator or speaker or character(s) cannot. Though it induces the elevated imaginative faculties of its readers, music in literature is both "always already worldly" (Benson) and everywhere tethered to what Kendall Walton calls the "work world," that is to say, the relevant artwork's imagined world—the dollhouse for the dolls.

James Baldwin's *If Beale Street Could Talk* (1974) is told by a first-person narrator who must, like many of Baldwin's late narrators (e.g. Hall Montana in *Just Above My Head*, Leo Proudhammer in *Tell Me How Long the Train's Been Gone*), fill in the gaps created by first-person limitations—that is to say, the narrator, Tish, must imagine, or at least imaginatively ornament, crucial scenes. In one such scene, Tish, now a Baldwin surrogate, delivers a close third-person account of her mother, Sharon, traveling to Puerto Rico to meet the woman, Victoria, who claims to have been raped by Tish's fiancé, Fonny, and convince her to retract her testimony. Once arrived, Sharon enters a nightclub—she's there to speak to Victoria's husband—and a band is playing. Because Tish (who was not present at the scene) narrates the story, she can decide, like a DJ or a novelist or Mr. West with his "musical telephone," what music her mother will hear, and Tish verily announces to the reader that the music ought to remind Sharon of her past: "If I remember 'Uncloudy Day' because I remember myself sitting on my mother's knee when I first heard it, she remembers 'My Lord and I': *And so, we'll walk together, my Lord and I*. That song is Birmingham, her father and her mother, the kitchens, and the mines." (Curiously, as a form of metafictional music, this might be a soundless example of non-diegetic sound.) The music therefore emboldens Sharon—echoes of home and family both accompany and fortify her—so that "she is alone merely physically, in the same way, for example, that she is alone when she goes shopping for her family. . . . she has a family to feed."

However, rather than forge solidarity between two ethnicities historically disenfranchised by the US judicial system (African Americans and Puerto Ricans), the music prefigures barriers separating Sharon and Victoria: it becomes a symbol for the complex racial, cultural, and political landmine yet lying between them. Just as Sharon's "only option is to play the American tourist"—she is, in Brian Norman's words, "unexpectedly thrust into an imperialist position"—so the Puerto Rican band can only bungle American music: "no one who had ever had a lover, a mother or father, or a Lord, could sound so despairingly masturbatory." Via Tish's imaginative reconstruction/ornamentation of Sharon's memory, Baldwin comments on the importance of black music as well as the sometimes painful ramifications of its popularity. As Ed Pavlić has written: "Sharon listens with one ear and, with the other, hears black music, black lives, being imitated." When the musicians who "know nothing at all about the song they are singing" and who may, in consequence, "know nothing about themselves at all" finish, "Sharon claps for them, because she prays for them." Blurring the divide between character, reader, and author, effectively pinch-hitting for his first-person narrator (Tish), Baldwin uses music as an intermediary linking the work world—the work world *within* the work world, in this case—to our own, even as that very music (as a social artifact) heralds the difficulties of transnational contact.

Outro (Vamp and Fade)

If only it could play you, too, tonight—
discordant instrument,
heart
— Eugenio Montale

And meanwhile, in Edward Bellamy's *Looking Backward*, in the evening, after *a lot* of conversation, Mr. West is escorted to a bedroom in which there is "a musical telephone," and he is shown how, "by turning a screw, the music could be made to fill the room, or die away to an echo so faint and far that one could scarcely be sure whether he heard or imagined it." West is tempted to listen to "the finest tunes in the world"—who wouldn't be?—but his host, a Doctor Leete, persuades him to sleep. Nevertheless, all across Boston, music remains awake, remains traveling from performance hall to telephone wire to private music room or bedroom, whether it can be heard or not . . .

a song that would tell the story of all these things together

100 NOTES ON 3 ALBUMS

1. Three extraordinary contributions to the longstanding collaboration between poetry and jazz:

Benjamin Boone & Philip Levine
The Poetry of Jazz
Origin Records, 2018

Nicole Mitchell & Haki R. Madhubuti
Liberation Narratives
TWP/ black earth music, 2017

Andrew Rathbun Large Ensemble
Atwood Suites
Origin Records, 2018

2. *On the fringes of the artworld, itself on the fringes of the world* . . . My father, a professional jazz trumpeter for over fifty years, heard not a peep about any of them.

3. I listen in my kitchen, on my decades-old Sony Walkman—5 a.m., full dark outside, my partner and kids still fast asleep—while my pour-over coffee drips into a mug.

4. Is the mind ever only in one place at a time?

5. There's a density to poetry-jazz collaborations: listeners cannot *not* assess (for better and for worse) the execution of each discipline on its own terms, even as the two function together and cannot be absorbed otherwise. "'We are two and we are one'" (Borges).

6. Listening to these albums, I develop a taste for such density. (Yet of course—for core practitioners as well as for listeners—density requires nimbleness, a mentally athletic ability to maneuver tight spaces, like a poet. Like a soloist bumping into a ten-fingered chord.) Not to mention a taste for the density of how and where and with/around whom I listen.

7. From room to room I carry my daughter's pink boombox. It emits a charming scratchiness, like a phonograph. Thus I listen as I wash dishes, as I fold laundry, as I shave my head in the bathroom mirror—

8. I listen in the car, taxiing my kids to school. My five-year-old daughter taps her knees to a few tunes—"Call It Music" (*The Poetry of Jazz*, Track 12), an homage to Charlie Parker featuring Greg Osby on alto sax—but is frightened by others, especially "By the Waters of the Llobregat " (Track 13), with its spare minor-thirds and -ninths, its intense, dirge-like piano octaves: "planets, dust motes, distant solar systems."

9. As its title suggests, Ralph Ellison's 1955 essay "Living with Music" explores the unusual, unexpected, and under-discussed ways in which music interacts with daily life, and vice

versa. So why has the ever-present, extra-musical aspect of listening largely evaded or been ignored by (non-John Cageophile) critics and reviewers?

10. Marvin Bell and Christopher Merrill recently published a book of poetic correspondence, *After the Fact: Scripts & Postscripts* (2016), whose working title was *Everything at Once*. Isn't that a great mantra—"Everything at once"—for an ideal method of listening?

11. Without the five-note opera-house bell that informed his audience to please find their seats, Keith Jarrett would never have "composed" the indelible opening phrase to *Köln Concert* (1975).

12. Boone's *The Poetry of Jazz* opens with "Gin"—a long swig of it for our late-lamented Philip Levine—and the tune's head, with its flat-fives and harmonic-minor trills, is appropriately celebratory. I listen as I tidy around the house this morning, and gradually I observe a swagger in my step, a wanna-be-cool energy that echoes the poem's youth, comedy, eagerness, naiveté—all of which are on display from Levine's opening tip: "The first time I drank gin / I thought it must be hair tonic."

13. The first time I read a Levine poem I thought it must've been written by a friend's dad or somebody. So down-to-earth it was, so straight-talking. "You stand in the rain in a long line / waiting at Ford Highland Park. For work," begins "What Work Is," probably his most famous poem. Only years

later, in college, when I began to write poems myself, did I understand that Levine's disarming colloquialism was one of his greatest strengths.

14. Madhubuti, too, is disarming—differently. On most tunes, Mitchell's band lays a groove like a big quilt spread for a picnic, and Madhubuti recites. He doesn't recite his poems melodramatically or with oracular fever/fervor. To the contrary, he recites with a clear and measured humility. Almost a majesty. "The minor cadences of despair change often to triumph and calm confidence," wrote W.E.B Du Bois of "The Sorrow Songs." I believe *Liberation Narratives* is much closer to the "The Sorrow Songs" than first meets the ear.

15. But don't get me wrong: there *is* drama, musical excitement. Like a solo full of risk and surprise, listeners of *Liberation Narratives* experience a reaffirmation of the impulses that led to the formation and continual reformation of jazz in the first place—impulses to challenge, expand, resist, and give the slip to dominant Western rhythmic and harmonic expectations.

16. Jazz, after all, arose not from a mere desire to be "different" or "in vogue," but rather from deep personal, social, and cultural unrest, from a desire to transform the musical boundaries that reflect and stand in as a microcosm for the boundaries created by society itself. Just as citizen-subjects challenge normative conventions in the world, so jazz musicians challenge normative conventions in their music.

For the cultural, racial, and nonbinary Other in general, and for African Americans in particular, jazz pushes back against the status quo, presents ulterior versions of (musical) reality and ways of being.

17. "The work is play for mortal stakes," writes Robert Frost in "Two Tramps in Mud Time"; and, in truth, I can think of no work—play or no play—that makes mortal stakes more palpable.

18. So disarming—yes—but *arming*, too. Madhubuti arms his community with pride: "the music was ours, the dance was ours, was ours"—a pride made all the more communal in and amongst Mitchell's band.

19. A common attribute of both *Liberation Narratives* and *The Poetry of Jazz* is an unpretentious, ego-less desire to communicate the relevant poetry's feelings and moods; to be an organism both bolstering and responding to Madhubuti's and Levine's voices, respectively, in real time.

20. In real time, I'm walking in flip-flops around my backyard, dictating this into my iPhone. *The Poetry of Jazz* is playing full-blast on the stereo in our bedroom but I can just barely hear it. I'm hoping to absorb it osmotically. *Can it inflect or infect my thoughts? Can it, perhaps, "reach the unconscious levels of the mind"* (Ellison)? I think of the Italian inventor Guglielmo Marconi, who believed sound never ceases but merely diminishes in volume ad infinitum; hence, with the right technology, he conjectured, all sound is recoverable. Drawn

to impossible projects, I suddenly believe myself a bolsterer of and a responder to this album, to all three of these albums. Also that Levine's actual voice still resonates somewhere far beneath the recorded one in our bedroom.

21. I listen in bed, sipping ginger tea.

22. "To make layers, / As if they were a steadiness of days," writes Robert Hass.

23. Still, with eyes closed, I'm someplace else. ("Still" as in *however*, as in *even now*, as in *not moving, not making a sound*.)

24. Dusk. I go for a run and listen on my iPod. The homes in my neighborhood vary radically: a southern ranch-style mansion is a half-block from a vine-choked trailer on cinderblocks; on a nearby street, a lemon-yellow Victorian is right next to an abandoned cabin whose front door creaks eerily open and closed, open and closed. It pleases me so much to hear Levine's poems in this setting because they're filled with interclass contact, not to mention the fusion of so-called "high" and "low" art—a feature succinctly summed up in the title of his 1972 poem "Angel Butcher." It's almost as though *The Poetry of Jazz* is issuing from each radically different house at the same time, same volume, totally synced.

25. Or am I drawn less to impossible projects than to adventure and risk-taking; to "perilous" decisions; to artists who, like the Wile E. Coyote, run straight off a cliff and then believe for several exhilarating seconds that they can fly?

26. Boone flies on soprano sax for quite a few exhilarating seconds on "They Feed They Lion"—one of many poems Levine wrote in response to the 1967 Detroit Rebellion. Appropriately, Boone doesn't fly above or beyond the semantic content of the poem; instead, he flies *into* it—a spirit embodying Levine's words ("From my five arms and all my hands / From my white sins forgiven, they feed") by doing its own rioting, sonically, in solidarity with the disenfranchised.

27. But perhaps I should replace "spirit" with "bird"—a *bird* embodying Levine's voice. After all, birds pepper this album like Stevens' blackbirds: Bird as in Yardbird ("it was a new creation / coming into being, like the music of Charlie Parker"); the sparrows and night-shift owls of "A Dozen Dawn Songs, Plus One" ("If I had / a Milky Way I'd share it / with the sparrows picking / about the piss-speckled / snow"); and of course Boone and his illustrious band and guests—all of them swooping and soaring and zipping in all directions. "Zip little silver birds like buckshot dimes" (Fred Chappell).

28. My partner stands behind me as I write at my desk. After a moment she says, "Another ornithology about jazz musicians, huh?"

29. But isn't the abundance of bird allusions fitting? Isn't jazz a space of freedom and proteanism—"the wings of an extraordinary liberty," to borrow a phrase from Frank O'Hara?

30. In "They Feed They Lion," there's a coupled anger to Levine's voice and Boone's playing. Yet there's also a sadness. Like the slipperiness between comedy and tragedy, this angry music-poem is on the verge of breaking—a scream about to crack in the throat.

31. At my grandfather's funeral, my dad asked me to play with him and for my sister to dance along. He wanted us to "say" something together. Improvisationally. He told me nothing more than the key: D minor. "Just play," he said. And what began as a ballad eventually crescendoed and fell, and again crescendoed and decrescendoed, and then crescendoed and then fell again—like Sisyphus and his boulder. In the end, my sister held a pose with outstretched arms, and my dad lowered his horn and blinked, returning from wherever it was he'd gone inside himself, eyes red-rimmed and brimming with tears. He was very, very sad—yet he'd all but screamed through his horn (and half looked like he was about to scream some more).

32. On my desk beside me sits Levine's *Selected Poems*, the 1984 copper-colored Atheneum edition, the one with the Egyptian swallow on the cover.

33. *The Poetry of Jazz* is an elegy and homage to Philip Levine who died of pancreatic cancer in 2015. But it's also an elegy and homage to a far more expansive web of artists alive and dead: Tom Harrell (trumpet) appears on "I Remember Clifford," an homage to Clifford Brown; Branford Marsalis (tenor sax) appears on "Soloing," an homage to Coltrane; Greg Osby (alto

sax) appears on "Call It Music," an homage to Charlie Parker; and Chris Potter (tenor sax) appears on "The Unknowable," an homage to Sonny Rollins. This is a project that celebrates and mourns life, both.

34. And yet the album strikes me less as sparrows, owls, or blackbirds than as white mourning doves.

35. I listen as I sweep the porch, organize the mail, make our daughter's bed, do pullups—

36. *Liberation Narratives* is likewise elegiac. In "Gwendolyn Brooks" (Track 3), for example, Madhubuti praises the great "lady 'negro poet,'" a former teacher of his—"how beautiful she was/is"—focusing particularly on the life-affirming reciprocity of Black community:

> ... & how she helped them
> & she came back with:
> how necessary they were and how
> they've helped her.

37. One might argue, too, that the Andrew Rathbun Large Ensemble's *Atwood Suites* is an elegy for Kenny Wheeler (trumpeter, flügelhornist, composer) who died in September 2014. In his liner notes, Rathbun tells us that he composed the "Power Politics Suite" (Tracks 4, 5, and 6) "with Kenny's sound and Luciana Souza's voice uppermost in my mind. . . . [W]ith Kenny's beautiful dark sound soaring over the ensemble." Intentionally or un-, Tim Hagan's flügelhorn elegizes Wheeler.

38. There was a white dove release at my grandfather's funeral. Though the entire family knew it was coming—my step-aunt makes a living raising and releasing doves for special events—nothing in that moment could de-charm the sudden explosion of wingbeats and scattering white.

39. Now, writing in my notebook and listening to the opening of Rathbun's "Two Islands I" (Track 1), that morning comes whirling back to me . . .

40. "In the swift whirl of time music is a constant, reminding us of what we were and of that toward which we aspire" (Ellison).

41. In a 2000 conversation at Columbia University (for "The Artistry of 'Pops': Louis Armstrong at 100"), Stanley Crouch once claimed that Ajax and Achilles were based on people like Louis Armstrong and Art Blakey—people with tremendous physical power and endurance. Levine was just such a person. (So are Atwood and Madhubuti, for that matter.) Since his death in 2015, I have missed the steady diet of Levine poems appearing in literary magazines. Then I read through *Best American Poetry 2017*, edited by Natasha Trethewey, and it contains a new Levine poem, "Rain in Winter." I read it and—because I've been listening to *The Poetry of Jazz* for months—I hear his voice, his *living* voice, with Boone's band.

42. Now I'm holding *Atwood Suites*, whose black-and-white cover features a single dove, spread-winged over a chainlink fence, in silhouette.

43. *Nachträglichkeit*. A neologism difficult to translate into English. It means something like "afterwardness," or "afterliness," and is Freud's theory that an experience, especially a trauma, can alter one's memories, one's very past. Was there even music that overcast morning when the doves flew toward their coop in midtown Sacramento (or toward that which we aspire)? I cannot be sure. But I know that I cannot see them released in my mind's eye without also hearing Atwood and Rathbun's "Two Islands Suite": "as usual, we watch for / omens, we are sad."

44. "Perhaps the enjoyment of music," wrote Ellison, "is always suffused with past experience."

45. "The Music of Time," "Soloing," and "Call It Music" (*The Poetry of Jazz,* Tracks 7, 8, and 12) are loungey tunes—lush chords and brushes and honeyed vibrato—but they're no-place lounges, edge-of-the-world lounges, liminal lounges, lounges at the threshold of paradise.

46. *On the fringes of the artworld, itself on the fringes of the world . . .*

47. *Atwood Suites*, however, isn't primarily an elegy; it's primarily a feminist performance of "failure"—the kind of failure Jack Halberstam explores in *The Queer Art of Failure*

(2011), "an art of unbecoming." An anti-capitalist critique of the success-failure paradigm, Halberstam's treatise lauds and analyzes the elation of—the optimism inherent in—"losing." Failure glimpses alternatives, "recognizes that alternatives are embedded already in the dominant." Put too succinctly, *Atwood Suites* attempts, in Halberstamian fashion, to "lose"—and thus to imagine "other goals for life, for love, for art, and for being."

48. Rathbun has musically entrapped the voice (Luciana Souza) embodying Atwood's poems. Just as the poems struggle with power politics ("If I love you // is that a fact or a weapon?"), so the vocals (speaker-heroine) struggle to evade or escape the clutches of the orchestra (the machine of patriarchy), thereby placing *Atwood Suites* in conversation with foundational feminist texts such as Kate Chopin's *The Awakening* (1899).

49. Under the bright green artificial stars of my son's turtle nightlight, I listen. Preparing for a lecture on 19th-century American literature, I listen.

50. A fin-de-siècle feminist novel, *The Awakening* is the story of Edna Pontellier, a young woman who, stifled by her bourgeois marriage and maternal responsibilities, falls in love with a man named Robert Lebrun while vacationing on Grand Isle. Robert, unwilling to disrupt the sanctity of a marriage, abruptly leaves for Mexico. Back home in New Orleans, Edna, lovesick for Robert, commences an affair with a disreputable Lothario named Alcée Arobin and moves into a

smaller house away from her husband. There she paints and enjoys her newfound independence. When Robert returns, Edna and he profess their love for one another, though Robert, still unable to disrupt a marriage, once again departs. He leaves a note behind: "I love you. Good-by—because I love you." Edna then returns to Grand Isle, where she swims far out to sea . . .

51. Bear with me. No: *bird* with me. *Everything-at-once* with me.

52. By swimming far out to sea, Edna Pontillier not only evades the patriarchy, her bourgeois marriage, and her maternal role in the nuclear family—she also evades the proto-realist terms to which she, as heroine, has been bound. Put simply, Edna's final act is less "suicide" as we understand it than a form of literary performance art—an extraordinary display of what Halberstam calls *radical passivity*, or "the willing giving over of the self to the other, to power." Like Dutch conceptual artist Bas Jan Ader's final performance, "In Search of the Miraculous" (1975), an attempt to sail across the Atlantic in a 6-foot-long sailboat ("a ridiculous toy," my friend d. tells me), Edna submits to the sensuous "touch of the sea" in order to stage her own unbecoming.

53. Because Atwood's embodied poems (Souza's voice) are composed, and therefore do not display the inescapable imperfection and occasional roughness of jazz improvisation, a remarkable claustrophobia is produced: the voice, confined to what's written, is exquisitely but all too politely displayed

before our ears. Lacking freedom and autonomy, the voice's melody talks one game ("There are two islands / at least, they do not exclude each other") but walks another. What we hear, then, in contradistinction to the relative freedom of the instrumentalists' solos—particularly Tim Hagan's flügelhorn solos—is the sound of confinement itself. We are denied female empowerment (or the possibility of it) through improvisation. Like Edna's submission to the sea, the singing performs *radical passivity*: it submits to written composition in order to stage its unbecoming. The vocalists' "failure" to actualize her autonomy, i.e. her improvisatory skills, only magnifies the listener's desire to behold—aurally—her freedom. By "quietly losing," to borrow a phrase from Halberstam, we cannot help but bring our feminist energies and empathy *to* this music. We want to compensate for what's lacking.

54. More specifically, we want Rathbun as composer to convert Souza's confinement (which might serve as a microcosm for the experience of women generally) into a gender-equal mini-nation—a radicalized musical sphere in which she, a New Woman entirely, can renounce her former self and activate her freedom via improvisation.

55. Ellison: "I had learned . . . that the end of all this discipline and technical mastery was the desire to express an affirmative way of life through its musical tradition, and that this tradition insisted that each artist achieve his creativity within its frame."

56. George Moses Horton: "She like a restless bird, / Would spread her wings, her power to be unfurl'd, / And let her songs be loudly heard, / And dart from world to world."

57. We'll excuse Ellison's use of the masculine pronoun, seeing as jazz was—and largely remains—an exclusive Boy's Club. Nevertheless, his view of artistic achievement within the jazz tradition is a strikingly apt description of what Souza's voice, in contradistinction to her instrumental counterparts (Hagan's flügelhorn and Bill Stewart's drums), "fails" to do. Souza no doubt possesses discipline and technical mastery, but she is denied their "end": no expression of "an affirmative way of life," no achievement of her "creativity within its frame." In their respective compositions, Atwood (in language) and Rathbun (in music) have done this for her.

58. In the final paragraph of *The Awakening*, Edna fragments or sheds her personhood:

> She looked into the distance, and the old terror flamed up for an instant, then sank again. Edna heard her father's voice and her sister Margaret's. She heard the barking of an old dog that was chained to the sycamore tree. The spurs of the cavalry officer clanged as he walked across the porch. There was the hum of bees, and the musky odor of pinks filled the air.

Here, Edna at first maintains both agency ("looked") and emotion ("terror"). By the second and third sentences, however, she merely "heard" events from her life. And by the fourth and fifth sentences, "she" has ceased to be involved at all. Free from the authorial domain of the novelistic world, Edna's now a passive and detached observer of what was once her life, and the final two sentences return to the fictional universe, *her* universe, without her. Because the future lies beyond the novel's—and the nation's—purview, Chopin casts readers backward, sans Edna, into scenes previously explored (her infatuation with the cavalry officer). This tactic highlights the spectatorship of reading and "make[s] feminism"—to borrow another phrase from Halberstam—"into an ongoing commentary on fragmentariness, submission, and sacrifice." Chopin's novel succeeds by embracing and transforming characteristics (passivity, submission, detachment) commonly associated with failure.

59. As James Baldwin writes in "Sonny's Blues": "deep water and drowning were not the same thing."

60. The second disc of *Atwood Suites* opens with "Fractured," a series of detached phrases or melodic islands, its own form of feminism as "commentary on fragmentariness, submission, and sacrifice." Chopin casts off Edna at the end of *The Awakening*, and Rathbun likewise casts off Atwood's embodied poems: when we return to the musical universe of *Atwood Suites*, when the fractured music is again united, we return without Atwood. From this point forward, no words are uttered, only wordless melodies, and the voice has been estranged, "replaced," the poetic speaker altogether re-bodied. (The voice on the second disc is Aubrey Johnson's.)

61. And yet the album would not exist without Atwood's poems: they are the inspiration for, the very source-material of, *Atwood Suites*. This is true even of the album's second, poem-less disc in which the sound of confinement, the sound of poetry's *and* improvisation's ghostly absences (i.e. Johnson's wordless melodies—a far cry from scat), is all the more deeply and tragically confined.

62. "A bird with a broken wing . . . beating the air above, reeling, fluttering, circling disabled down, down, to the water" (Chopin).

63. A far cry, too, from either *Liberation Narratives* or *The Poetry of Jazz*, the music of which tends not to stray for too long without Madhubuti's or Levine's voices, respectively. (In fact, several Boone-Levine tunes are only a minute or so in length: "Making Light of It" [Track 2; 1:46]; "Arrival" [Track 9; 1:36].) *Atwood Suites*, then, is simultaneously an homage to Atwood's poems and a dramatized "failure" to actualize those poems in a jazz context—a power politics, indeed.

64. In the "Power Politics Suite," melodies are often doubled in voice and instrument (flügelhorn or tenor sax), like a locked embrace. Like the two figures on the bottom righthand corner of Atwood's 1996 reissue of *Power Politics: Poems* (1971): an androgynous mythological figure battling what appears to be a small hippopotamus. In any event, seeing as instruments solo and voices do not, we all know who's in control.

65. "This is not a house, there are no doors, / get out while it is / open, while you still can" (Atwood).

66. Whereas *Liberation Narratives* challenges gender inequality (in "Gwendolyn Brooks," in "Woman Black" [Track 9], to say nothing of Ugochi's vocals or Nicole Mitchel's inimitable flute-playing), *Atwood Suites* dramatizes it.

67. Employing his voice as a poet *and* as a musician, Madhubuti enlarges my conception of jazz and of "jazz poetry." We all know language is its own music; music, its own language. Yet Madhubuti becomes at times a member of the rhythm section, syncopating, creating polyrhythms. There's also a crucial second voice in *Liberation Narratives*—the vocalist Ugochi. In "Gwendolyn Brooks," after Madhubuti recites a percussive litany of *blacks*—"black doubleblack purpleblack blueblack been black was / black daybeforeyesterday blackerthan ultrablack"—Ugochi echoes him, first in song and then in speech. An almost random double recitation. "[J]azz players actively *resist* formal coherence," writes jazz scholar Lee B. Brown. And then finally, adding fuel to the tune's already rhythmically vertiginous fire, Madhubuti recites with a delay effect, so that even his repeated words are themselves repeated—echo of an echo of an echo, echoing down a long hall of what feels like history.

68. In college, before the ubiquity of mp3s, YouTube, Spotify, et al., I bought a second small stereo for the express purpose of playing two albums simultaneously. Steve Reich's *Different Trains* and Coltrane's *Blue Train*. David Shire's score of *The*

Taking of Pelham One Two Three and Prez's "Taking a Chance on Love." *Same time, same volume, totally synced.* I wanted to be a composer, and I thought the experiment might release in me some nascent, groundbreaking originality.

69. When I run and listen to these three poetry-jazz collaborations, I find myself unconsciously accelerating or decelerating so that my footsteps land on the downbeats. But not during "Gwendolyn Brooks."

70. Ugochi and Madhubuti's stunning call-and-response in that tune—not unlike Levine and Harrell at the close of "I Remember Clifford" (*The Poetry of Jazz*, Track 6)—is worlds apart from Hagan's solos alongside the musical captivity of Souza's voice in either the "Two Islands" or the "Power Politics" suites (*Atwood Suites*, Tracks 1-6).

71. Chopin's *The Awakening* famously opens with a caged, green-and-yellow parrot.

72. I often remind my students that texts are not "products," despite the fact that their words on their pages/cages are unalterable. *A text*, I tell them, *is an experience—and quite an active one at that*. Of course, jazz musicians and enthusiasts need not be reminded, accustomed as they are to experiencing art as it happens, to being present with it in real time. "Music is a time-oriented art," said Maria Schneider. "So it's how you play a person's attention through time." It should go without saying, then, that these three albums make activity—make *hyper*-activity—of poetry.

73. Madhubuti's poems strike me as the most active, the most purposefully active—not to mention *activist*. "This collaboration is twenty-seven years in the making, a mere teardrop in this universe," he writes in the liner notes to *Liberation Narratives*, "and hopefully represents an invitation for you to think outside the confines of America's provincialism."

74. In Julian Schnabel's 1996 biopic *Basquiat,* Jean-Michel Basquiat (Jeffrey Wright) paints a streak of white paint across the underbelly of one of Warhol's (David Bowie's) two identical black stenciled Pegasuses. Warhol, looking on, says in his endearingly whiny voice, "Ahh, gee, Jean, that was my favorite part." Later, the pop artist stencils an AMOCO logo, which Basquiat promptly scrawls out with a violet oil stick—a long strikethrough and a series of steep Vs. The points of an upturned SAMO crown? Warhol: "What are you doing? You're painting out everything I do." Basquiat then paints white words ("JELLO," "NERVOUS SYST M") on the opposite Pegasus, in addition to red flames spewing out of its muzzle.

76. Whether I watch this scene or listen to *Liberation Narratives,* the same synapses fire in my brain.

75. At the Georgia Institute of Technology, Dr. Caroline Young taught a course called "Rendering *Tender Buttons*." In lieu of assignments intended to facilitate comprehension of Gertrude Stein's seminal text, Young urged students to respond creatively through the visual and performing arts—a process sometimes referred to as "intersemiotic translation."

77. Though the sea has long been a stage for exploration and travel, such explorations are largely tied to capitalist enterprise (Melville's *Moby-Dick*) or survival (Crane's "The Open Boat"). In Chopin's *The Awakening*, however, the sea is of another order—a powerful, seductive, erotic force beckoning Edna throughout the book with this refrain: "The touch of the sea is sensuous, enfolding the body in its soft, close embrace." Hence, the sea is an escape from the authorial domain of fiction and into an uninhabitable, non-national space (here, too, the same synapses fire in my brain)—an invitation to think outside the confines of America's provincialism, indubitably:

78. Like Chopin's Orphic, ulterior sea, Madhubuti and Ugochi's voices (unlike Souza and Johnson's, or Souza and Hagan's, in *Atwood Suites*) glimpse the power of alternative imaginaries:

> Spaced from the old thoughts into
> the new. Zooomm. Zoooommmmm. Zooommmmmm.
> click.
> design yr own neighborhoods,   Zoom   it can be,
> teach yr own children,   Zoom   Zoom   it can be,
> build yr own loop,   Zoom   Zoom   it can be,
> feed yr own people.   Zoom   Zoom   it can be

The selfsame imagination with which George Jackson counseled his brother, Jonathan, April 14, 1969:

> You can make your own bench cheap. Buy or find or take from someone a 6′ × 15″ board, rather thick and heavy, say 2″ at least. Tack on some old surplus army blankets and that's it. You then simply lay your board on top of three wooden horses, old wooden milk crates, or any strong or reinforced wood boxes, or stretch it between two chairs. Leave it unattached, however, because that way you can use it for incline presses by leaning it against the wall, or letting it rest one end on the ground, one on your box or chair.

79. Mornings, on the way to his preschool, rather than cry or sing or take off his shoes and toss them at the back of my head, my two-old-year-old son will listen to Madhubuti with uncharacteristic attention, gazing out the window.

80. Listening to Madhubuti as I walk the aisles of our local Kroger grocery store, I feel spewing out behind me the sonic flame-red paint of *Liberation Narratives*, rich with musical thrust-and-parry, rich with Madhubuti's deep social intelligence: "we goin a need mo than wine bottles, promises & ray gun dreamin."

81. In Kroger, too, I recite to myself the well-known opening sentence of Ellison's "Living with Music": "In those days it was either live with my music or die with noise, and we chose rather desperately to live."

82. *Liberation Narratives* validates, improves upon, and provides a soundtrack for my own feelings and inner commentary. It clarifies, it makes tangible, it makes us nod our heads.

83. I listen as I walk across campus, as I walk upstairs and down the hall and into my Intro to Creative Writing class. Then I listen *with* my class.

84. Jazz is a social art. Poetry is, too, of course—"All words require a shared experience," wrote Borges—but jazz is doubly social: there's the conversation among the musicians *and* the conversation they're having (alone and together) with their audience. Naturally, then, the conversations that can and do occur when the two disciplines are combined are manifold and frequently chaotic, like Einstein's hair.

85. "If you can't stop a hurricane," says Madhubuti in "Move Into Our Own" (Track 2), "be one."

86. My instinct is to pluralize (or generate a hurricane out of) an artwork's potential meanings, so that it cannot be reduced to mere neat takeaways, and so that its admirers will retain their interest in and curiosity about it—forever.

87. Can I say I want you to love these three albums forever?

88. Are all critical essays also (to varying degrees) aesthetic essays?

89. Speaking of questions. On the way to her soccer practice, my daughter yells from her car seat, "What's he saying? Why's he talking to that saxophone?"

90. I listen to Rathbun's "Fractured," the opening cut to the second disc of *Atwood Suites,* as I piece together these disparate vignettes.

91. I listen to "A Dozen Dawn Songs, Plus One" (*The Poetry of Jazz,* Track 10) while my car goes through the drive-thru car wash—and it's the most pleasurable experience of my day. It brings me indescribable happiness.

92. In a late chapter of Jackie Kay's *Trumpet* (1998), Colman—adopted son of legendary jazz trumpeter Joss Moody—remembers his father telling stories with his horn:

> As a treat sometimes, he would ask for ingredients to his story. Everyone present had to give one. Whatever you could think up. A butterfly. A chest. A little girl looking through a keyhole. Hair. A baby ape. An old woman in a house by the sea. And then he would make up a song on his trumpet, a song that would tell the story of all these things together, and sometimes it was possible for each person to recognize the music of the butterfly, of the wooden house, of the little girl.

Similarly, in Baldwin's "Sonny's Blues," during Sonny's climactic final solo, a wave of seemingly private images (not unlike the wave of images Chopin invokes in dismantling Edna) washes over the narrator-brother:

> I saw my mother's face again, and felt, for the first time, how the stones of the road she had walked on must have bruised her feet. I saw the moonlit road where my father's brother died. And it brought something else back to me, and carried me past it, I saw my little girl again and felt Isabel's tears again, and I felt my own tears begin to rise.

The personal, in both of these texts, *is* social. Music's "private" conjuring unites us, enlarges our empathy. "Sonny's fingers filled the air with life, his life," writes Baldwin. "But that life contained *so many others*" (my emphasis).

93. Jazz, more so than any other genre of music, is relational—a web of interconnectivity.

94. "[A]n ecstasy of rhythm and memory and brassy affirmation of the goodness of being alive and part of the community" (Ellison).

95. For this reason, *The Poetry of Jazz* is most compelling when Levine references jazz musicians in his poems, when he injects the still-jiving phantom sound of long-dead artists into recent recordings, so that Bird or Coltrane or Clifford Brown plays in our imaginations, in our memories, right alongside Greg Osby or Branford Marsalis or Chris Potter—a musical palimpsest.

96. In a recent essay on "soul in music," Ed Pavlić writes, "The basic dilemma is that between individuality and community. Lyrically speaking, that's the *introspective* (seeing within) versus what I call the *inter-spective* (seeing between)." For me, all three of these poetry-jazz collaborations richly incite private (and not-so-private) images capable of uniting us and enlarging our empathy; images in which we see, or rather *hear*, the vital connections we maintain for one another and that jazz and poetry traditions maintain for themselves across time; images that do indeed fill the air with life—my life—your life—lives that fundamentally contain so many others.

97. I listen as the sun breaks over my neighbors' treetops.

98. As Ashbery writes in "The System": "At this time of life whatever being there is is doing a lot of listening."

99. "[A] song that would tell the story of all these things together" (Kay).

100. I listen in a lounge, with my interspective arms outstretched, at the edge of the world.

I'd sing you a song if I could sing

ART & ARTIFICE IN ELLEN DOUGLAS'S *CAN'T QUIT YOU, BABY*

Ah, well, I didn't say it was possible. I said, Try.
—E.D.

Ellen Douglas's *Can't Quit You, Baby* (1988) is a prismatic and profoundly subtle novel. And yet, despite its impressive mélange of competing voices and points of view, strategies and techniques, styles and modes—all of which forces readers to approach the narrative from a variety of angles—the novel's prose and central action quietly belie its ambition. Ostensibly, *Can't Quit You, Baby* is about the fraught, longtime relationship of a white mistress, Cornelia, and her African American housekeeper, Julia (nicknamed Tweet), in Civil Rights-era Mississippi. But the novel is in fact as much about the narrator's—the "tale-teller's"—struggle to tell a tale that can transcend racial barriers (or is at least capable of it) and at last bring these two women together as true friends, true equals. Such is the layered, pluralistic nature of this novel. Douglas is a magician of novelistic multitasking, and I say "magician" because the multiple, simultaneous tasks are often in contention with one another: the ostensible plot, for example, largely falls under the tradition of realist mimetic fiction, whereas the metafictive tale-teller, among other features, is a staple of postmodern fiction—that is to say, fiction (post-WWII) that employs pastiche, incorporates (often self-consciously and -referentially) a number of divergent styles/traditions, and in some way fractures or challenges the coherence of a single reliable version of a narrative. In brief, this essay will discuss a variety of ways in which *Can't Quit You, Baby* struggles with and against itself; how it both offers and remains skeptical of racial reconciliation, interrogating and embracing the potential for change; how it paradoxically succeeds by failing; how it frees itself from the "illusion of freedom"; and how it—like Bernard Malamud's *The Tenants* (1971)[1]—functions within and at the same time abandons the conventions of popular realist mimetic fiction.

Before moving forward, however, it's important to note what "racial barriers" means in the context of this essay, which is precisely, if only partly, what it means in the world at large: it means that "racism is ordinary," a tenet critical race theorists have long proclaimed. With the exception of the assassination of Martin Luther King, Jr—an historical tragedy that, in the novel, given the emotional vulnerability such an event engenders, ushers in a scene of potential connection and/or intimacy between Tweet and Cornelia—the racial barriers discussed in this essay, the conflicts *Can't Quit You, Baby* attempt (for these two women, at least) to overcome, are not shocking, barefaced discriminations, but rather Cornelia's continual rehearsal, however unconscious, of quotidian racism, that "system of formalized distortions of thought," to borrow a phrase from Patricia J. Williams, that underpin our daily lives: untold microaggressions; legal rationalizations; feelings of moral or intellectual or civic superiority. As Suzanne W. Jones states in "Writing Southern Race Relations: Stories Ellen Douglas Was Brave Enough to Tell": "Cornelia, whom Douglas marks physically as hard of hearing, politely listens to Tweet's stories about white injustice and black hardship, marital infidelity and familial competition over land. But Cornelia does not hear in these stories the evidence of institutionalized racism in the town's law offices and banks that Ellen Douglas makes sure her readers discern." So long as such underpinnings are upheld, so long as Cornelia fails to discern as well as acknowledge the "ordinary racism" that circumscribes their lives, our two protagonists remain distant strangers; as in Magritte's *L'Assassin Menace* (which I'll discuss later and which appears in chapter five of the novel), the two women remain—despite their physical proximity to one another—in separate spheres, inauspiciously nonintegrated; indeed, unintegrable.

Let us begin, plainly, with an examination of the style and technical features of Douglas's prose, so entwined with the book's subject matter, the most striking and indeed crucial of which is the omission of quotation marks. This at once equalizes or democratizes the language of *Can't Quit You, Baby*. That is to say, the novel refuses to make any qualitative or hierarchical distinctions between dialogue and narrative, between black and white, between speech and song, between past (tense) and present (tense), between thought and action. This feature seems akin to the refusal among, say, Mexican-American "code-switching" writers, such as poets Juan Felipe Herrera, Jose Montoya or Eduardo C. Corral, to italicize Spanish, refusing in other words to subordinate Spanish to English. But perhaps more interestingly, the omission of quotation marks facilitates Douglas's effortless movement between voices and styles.

Consider the following passage—from the pivotal fifth chapter in New York City—in which Cornelia believes Tweet is telepathically guiding her through her grief, as well as through the many quotidian practicalities—"Look out! Right there by that next pile of snow—right in front of you. Dog shit. Whoa!"—that she could, before the death of her husband, dreamily ignore: "You're in Harlem, Mrs. O'Kelly," Tweet says. "Plenty people here who'd kill you in a minute. Toss up a apple. Shoot out the core. Peel it and slice it before it hit the floor. Get on the next train. Don't even cross over the crosswalk and try to catch a southbound train. This platform's empty. Stay here and. . ./ A northbound train is roaring into the station." Here, "Tweet's voice" begins by locating Cornelia in Harlem and letting her know, albeit hyperbolically, that she, the upper-middle-class white woman, is now in the minority. The following three sentences—"Toss up a apple. Shoot out the core. Peel it and slice it before it hit the floor"—are likely, given their rhyme, song lyrics, something perhaps her grandpa might have sung—"My grandpa might be singing this: What set Paul and Silas free is good enough for you and me," she says elsewhere—intended to frighten Cornelia. Returning to guidance, to her role as disembodied fairy godmother, "Tweet" then retains the imperative mode: "Get on the next train. Don't even cross over the crosswalk and try to catch a southbound train." Lastly, "Tweet's" interior monologue melts via ellipses into narrative action: "Stay here and. . ./ A northbound train is roaring into the station." In short, the narrative slips seamlessly between three, or three-and-a-half, narrative voices—interior monologue, song lyrics, interior monologue with songlike echoes, and exterior action—all in just under seventy words.

Even still, *Can't Quit You, Baby* doesn't feel exactly postmodern; despite its range of styles and voices, it lacks the playfulness of postmodern classics like Italo Calvino's *If on a winter's night a traveler* (1979), the mythopoetic culture-clashing of Randall Kenan's *A Visitation of Spirits* (1989), the labyrinthine absurdity of Paul Auster's *New York Trilogy* (1985-1986), or the hypermodernity of, say, Don DeLillo's *White Noise* (1985). And yet there are a number of postmodern strategies employed throughout the novel, and chief among them is the tale-teller's intermittent "intrusions": the tale-teller (simultaneously an author and a figure of deauthorization) will at times *talk out* the telling of the story to the reader, exploring her self-consciousness, her insecurities, her inability or lack of authority to tell this story, essentially discovering how to tell the story even as it's being told: "What is it I want to tell you to make these tales plain?" This is why Matthew Luter and other critics have aptly described the narrator as "metafictive"—a narrator who essentially breaks the fourth wall and reveals the artificiality of her narrative— though it's worth noting that *Can't Quit You, Baby* is hardly a quintessential metafictional postmodern text.

Indeed, the novel does not set out to be either metafictional or postmodern, in the way that a Calvino novel clearly does, despite Douglas herself explaining in the opening chapter that the tale-teller is not herself, even if they share—*must share*—many similarities: "You may have assumed," for example, "that she is a white woman." On the contrary, the metafictive strategies ("intrusions," a false epiphany, the disclosure of the novel as artifice, etc) employed throughout are in the service of realism, albeit a realism that cannot or does not yet exist—a reality in which Cornelia and Tweet overcome racial barriers. Douglas cannot write a realist novel that reconciles the racial, socioeconomic tensions between her two protagonists because such reconciliation is, at least in her own hands, utterly unrealistic; and she refuses to present an unrealistic version of their story that might too easily—offensively—comfort a white audience all too anxious to ignore or forget racism altogether: "[The tale-teller] must resist the temptation to satisfy her sense of how Tweet and Cornelia *ought* to behave; must resist the need to keep herself comfortable." Rather than the presentation of an aesthetic, then, the postmodern strategies employed in *Can't Quit You, Baby* are mere practical solutions to the limitations of realist mimetic fiction, which simply cannot present an ulterior version of the world.

One more note about this tale-teller. She is often described as "intrusive," a pejorative (and therefore inaccurate) description, as though she is a proverbial third wheel, implying that the novel could have unfolded well enough without her—or else that the reader ought to fall so deeply into the story so as to forget that he or she is reading altogether—even if most readers and critics agree that her "intrusions" (her musings and interrogations) artfully complicate the book. As Susan V. Donaldson states in her essay "A Stake in the Story": "Douglas's third-person narrator...raises periodic questions about her authority as a storyteller, her descriptions of the main characters, her readers' expectations, and the ethics of narrating stories across racial lines." Furthermore, the tale-teller's struggle to tell this tale, to maneuver around and across the ethics of racial and socioeconomic boundaries, is as much a palpable conflict, a cause for readerly investment, as Cornelia and Tweet's vexed relationship. By folding her failures (her inability to write a realist mimetic story free of interrogation) into the fabric of the narrative itself, Douglas makes the tale-teller's desires and struggles an ancillary or even a contrapuntal plot. The tale-teller is less the third wheel than the necessary third note of a chord.

Can't Quit You, Baby belongs in my view to a not-so-fashionable brand of realism exhibited in, for instance, James Alan McPherson's "Elbow Room." This short story — the title story of McPherson's 1978 Pulitzer prize-winning collection of stories — follows the marriage and impending parenthood of a white man, Paul Frost, and a black woman, Virginia Valentine; and it is a narrative frequently and disturbingly interrupted by a nameless editor who — in italics — interrogates both the story and the narrator, repeatedly insisting on more explanation and clarity: *"Analysis of this section is needed. It is too subtle and needs to be more clearly explained."* Unlike Douglas's tale-teller, who complicates and deepens the often unspecific, unsatisfying plot points of *Can't Quit You, Baby*, McPherson's editor remains, in Charles Baxter's description, "obtuse about the complexities of racism, narration, identity, and storytelling, and has wanted these matters wrapped up and commodified, as if for an anthology to be used for pedagogical purposes... To the degree that the story resists that packaging, it gives back to its events the dignity of their own complexity." Compellingly, Ellen Douglas here inverts McPherson's tactic: she presents the commodified narrative, and then her metafictive narrator (along with a quartet of artistic references, which I'll soon discuss) infiltrates it, restoring to Tweet and Cornelia's events "the dignity of their own complexity."

Despite the many technical and stylistic achievements discussed above, *Can't Quit You, Baby* is finally a record failure, and I believe this failure is in fact the novel's greatest achievement. How can Douglas, a southern white woman, possibly write a novel that reconciles the relationship between even one white mistress and her black "help" in Civil-Rights-era Mississippi? After all, Douglas understands that her novel has ethical, real-life implications, that it will no doubt be read as a microcosm of racial tension in general (or at least in the south), and that she is therefore unequal to her art's demands. Nevertheless, as John Koethe writes in "Poetry and the Structure of Speculation," "the awareness of the futility of a conception may lead to an even greater insistence on it." While sympathetic to and familiar with failure as a fundamental element of art-making, Douglas refuses to grow bitter or to throw in the towel, and instead clings to the very idealism—to the failed story, to her original, idealistic vision of the story, the story of Cornelia and Tweet at last crossing racial boundaries and becoming true friends—that her tale-teller continually interrogates. "Under certain circumstances," Jack Halberstam writes in *The Queer Art of Failure*, "failing, losing, forgetting, unmaking, undoing, unbecoming, not knowing may in fact offer more creative, more cooperative, more surprising ways of being in the world." Put another way, by acknowledging the inevitable failure of her vision, Douglas is able to project a world capable of overcoming racism (the conclusion is clearly hopeful, clearly optimistic) and to suggest at the same moment its unlikeliness, seeing as its source—herself—is incapable of convincingly building such a world. The novel doesn't simply unburden its white audience. Indeed, the interchange of mimetic storytelling and metafictive interrogation (wherein the failure is admitted) rescues the novel, makes it an artistic success: the reader senses Douglas's unshakable desire for the book, and for society at large, to be what it is not and perhaps alas may never be: a world capable of transcending racism.

Boldly, willfully, Douglas attempts to tell a story that cannot be told, not unlike Canadian poet M. NourbeSe Philip's attempt to tell a story that cannot be told in *Zong!* (2008)—a book about the slave ship Zong, whose captain ordered one-hundred-and-fifty Africans thrown overboard in 1781. *Zong!* is principally an erasure of the two-page summary of *Gregson v. Gilbert* (the trial that followed the horrific event) wherein not only sentences but words themselves are fractured—"not so much a recombinant narrative," writes Philip in the book's closing essay, "as a recombinant antinarrative. The story that can't ever be told." Philip distorts found material—she finds the words, the "pure utterance," within extant words and phrases, those "legal fictions and norms that supported and emerged from the institution of slavery," as Anthony Reed notes in *Freedom Time: The Poetics and Politics of Black Experimental Writing* (2014):

                         ... in i a

  m wit

     hout sin b   ut we me

         et be

    come friend

```
        s sea fa
                        ns dance se
    a cre
        atu                             res ride the b
            ones we rest
they re                         sist . . .
```

—whereas Douglas distorts the predictable well-trod realist narrative of racial reconciliation (Kathryn Stockett's bestselling 2009 novel *The Help* is a recent example) she herself has written, behind a persona, so as to realistically enact what cannot, or not yet, be enacted.

Before we switch our attention to Cornelia—one of the great accomplishments of this novel—it's important to note the characterological success of Tweet and to explain why she is not at the center of this essay. After all, Tweet's buoyant plucky indelible voice carries roughly the first half of this narrative. Readers become voyeurs as Tweet tells the unlistening, untalkative Cornelia the story of her own childhood and marriage. Because Cornelia is so vacant, so without personhood at all, Tweet is forced to overcompensate: she (with a little help from our tale-teller) must propel her silent potential friend through the early stages of the novel. This is not only heroic but, from Douglas's point of view, a sign of respect for her ability and right to tell her own story. The self-confidence Tweet displays therein is crucial, too. Though she changes (or is at least capable of change) by novel's end, Tweet is confident and knowing, refreshingly opinionated even—she is appalled by John's funeral preparations, for example: "And a little two-bit social security coffin. No flowers. I wouldn't bury a dog like that"—from page one. Douglas is unwilling to tinker with Tweet's life and consciousness; it would be an unethical transgression that is also, as a result of Tweet's verisimilitude (the accuracy of her dialect, the nuance of her emotions, the particularity of her past, etc), largely unnecessary. Unlike Cornelia, who lives merely in her own mind and is in consequence detached from everything, Tweet is a successful realist character, quite at home in the novel's "real world," quite aware of her own problems and the problems of others—Cornelia's in particular. For this reason, despite our investment in Tweet, despite her strength and three-dimensionality as a character, *Can't Quit You, Baby* is finally less Tweet's story than it is Cornelia's, since Tweet is smarter, more capable, more experienced, and her need to change over the course of the narrative is therefore far less crucial.

But who is Mrs. Cornelia O'Kelly? She is on the one hand a stereotypical mid-twentieth-century housewife who cooks, makes jam, arranges flowers, and talks sparsely and vapidly—rather like Evan S. Connell's Mrs. Bridge who, in her eponymous 1959 novel, refuses to tackle issues of race, gender, and class in Kansas City, Missouri, between the two World Wars. On the other hand, because her inner life is so off-limits, because we don't have access at all to her thoughts and emotions—"I am left therefore with surfaces, with scenes," the tale-teller confesses—Cornelia piques our curiosity. To answer the above question, I think we ought to begin with her childhood—that is to say, with chapter two.

Chapter two largely relates the "fairytale" courtship of Cornelia and John, and echoes the fairybook-obsessed childhood of Anna Anderson, protagonist of Douglas's debut novel *A*

Family's Affairs (1961).² Cornelia lives with her mother, Mrs. Wright, a hideous archetypal fairytale witch—she "looks like a fat spider, with her swelling body and hairy arms and legs," her face "caked, in the style of the forties, with too much pancake makeup"—on the third story of "an octagonal tower clad in fish-scale shingles," "windowed in the east and south and surrounded by a captain's walk." This "captain's walk" not only heightens the dreamy solitude and virginal preservation of Cornelia, our faux princess, our faux Rapunzel—"What could be more romantic than the sight of a young girl sitting in the morning sunshine in her tower bedroom brushing her hair?"—but also seems, by its very military name, to already belong to her beloved John O'Kelly, an American pilot and "certified hero" who at the time of their meeting works as an American Army Air Corps instructor "teaching other young men to avoid death as he had." The remainder of this chapter unfolds in typical fairy tale fashion: Cornelia, courted by John, opposes her mother's demands that she not see him—by chapter's end, Mrs. Wright has even locked her up in the tower—and implicitly runs away with her "prince" anyway.

Why did Douglas write this chapter as a fairy tale? I would argue that the chief reason is she wanted to juxtapose Cornelia's idyllic youth to Tweet's largely brutal youth; the fairy tale analog for Tweet is, importantly, the frightening "Hansel and Gretel": "Remember? How the father accedes to the wicked stepmother's urging and with her leads the two children deep into the forest and leaves them there to die." But Douglas wants the reader to suspect—as indicated by my use of scare quotes ("fairytale") in the opening sentence of the preceding paragraph—the veracity of

Cornelia's past. More specifically, Douglas *wants* the reader to interrogate her past: Was she really as isolated as Rapunzel, as dreamy as a fairytale princess? Was their courtship really as romantic and simple (not to mention as superficial and sanitized) as the happily-ever-after "translations" of, say, original German fairy tales? Or, conversely, are we reading Cornelia's *memory* of her and John's courtship? In the end, however, I suppose it doesn't matter whether Cornelia truly experienced a romantic fairy tale as a young woman or merely gazed back on her and John's courtship through rose-tinted glasses. After all, fairy tale or no, Cornelia lives the bulk of her adult life in a fantasy—"Maybe in her fond ignorance, her foolish trust, she has lived her whole life in a false, an imaginary world"—adopting the role of queen; as our tale-teller asks us early in the novel: "Did you notice that she stands slightly swayback, as if she's lifted her shoulders like a queen ready to receive the heavy, ermine-trimmed mantle she must wear to the coronation?"

Thus Cornelia's interior, emotional life does not correspond to reality. Having lived in her imagination, in her fantasies, all her life, Cornelia is metaphorically blind and quite literally deaf—she often just turns off her hearing aid—to the world around her. "She neither hears nor sees," writes Wordsworth in "A Slumber did my Spirit Seal," a poem that Cornelia thinks about later in the novel and that I will soon discuss. Importantly, Tweet and her family (all of whom appear by contrast intensely self-aware) are very wise to her self-delusion, her fantastic ignorance of everything: her family, for example, keeps secrets from her for many years (Andrew's wife and stepchildren, Sarah's marijuana habit, and so on). Indeed, Douglas provides us again and again with scenes in which Cornelia is confronted with reality but refuses to perceive it—most touchingly, I think, when John, perhaps emboldened by his pre-stroke "drunkenness," "cupped his two hands, made rings of his thumbs and forefingers, held them up to his eyes like binoculars, scanning the heavens. You so far away, he said. Far away. You ever coming back?" In part, this novel is about Cornelia's "coming back,"[3] about her opening her eyes, at last turning up the volume on her hearing aid, and for that reason Tweet emerges as the novel's true heroine: "Why is it that Tweet is the only one who raises her voice and tells Cornelia what is really going on?"

Cornelia's decision to stay at her friend Evelyn's New York City apartment—her decision to "learn to be alone"—connects with the mention of Wordsworth some eight pages earlier. After the death of John, the grief-stricken Cornelia stays briefly with her son Andrew, where she wanders around in nature, "on the land across the river from Baton Rouge," living in a kind of trance, so absorbed is she in her own fantasy-infused memories—a potent hallucinogen indeed. It is fitting, then, that—after she cuts her hand and "stumbles down the slope out onto the willow flat below," then simply lies there for a while in the willow leaves, feeling herself sinking—the poet she thinks about is William Wordsworth: "She would sink downward toward the earth's center, toward John, where he lay—like in the poem, she thought—rolled round, rolled round—the words rolled in her head—rolled round with rocks and stones and trees...." The poem is Wordsworth's "A Slumber did my Spirit Seal":

> A slumber did my spirit seal;
>   I had no human fears:
> She seemed a thing that could not feel
>   The touch of earthly years.
>
> No motion has she now, no force;
>   She neither hears nor sees;
> Rolled round in earth's diurnal course,
>   With rocks, and stones, and trees.

"She" is in truth Lucy Gray, a fictional character of desire and loss for the speaker of this and Wordsworth's four other "Lucy Poems," much like Michael Furey is a character of desire and loss for Gretta in James Joyce's "The Dead," referenced in chapter five. Yet in the context of *Can't Quit You, Baby*, "she" becomes, of course, Cornelia; and in addition to powerfully describing Cornelia's own grief—an utter indifference to the world, an utter surrender to death (though she is scarcely hurt at all physically)—the poem also functions as a hinge between her hallucinatory, grief-stricken wandering and her desire to be alone, "to learn to be alone," in New York City. After all, Wordsworth is the prototypical poet both of nature (the Lake District inspired much of *The Preludes*, for example) and of solitude (as in his most famous poem, "I Wander Lonely as a Cloud"). And yet Wordsworth is also, contrapuntally, an ideal contrast to Cornelia; in the words of scholar John Hughes, "Wordsworth, as a poet, was someone for whom humanity and nature were always to be disclosed and rediscovered, never to be assumed." In short, it is not coincidental that Cornelia's first decision, post John's death—"I *will* be alone. That's it. I will learn to be alone"—is informed or influenced or at least inflected by Wordsworth. Importantly, too, Cornelia's receptivity to fantasy, her ability to be influenced by (among other things) art, is crucial in setting the stage for her series of "art experiences"—or perhaps I should say *experiments*—in New York City, in chapter five.

Chapter five is the novel's most pivotal chapter. Even so, its central action—Cornelia's journey to and subsequent "rebirth" in New York—what Karen J. Jacobsen has aptly called her "feminist awakening"—has been largely misunderstood. In brief, this is what happens in New York City: Cornelia arrives, studies René Magritte's *L'Assassin Menace* in the Museum of Modern Art, sees Ingmar Bergman's *Persona* in a nearby theater, begins to hear "Tweet's voice" in her mind, slips on the ice and hurts her head, is nursed by a mover who reminds her of a childhood crush (a boy named Lewis Robinson) and with whom she has a one-night stand, is informed that Tweet has had a seizure at the stove and severely burned herself—"they called in a neurologist," says Cynthia, Tweet's daughter-in-law—and at last returns to Mississippi, a new woman, to help Tweet convalesce. Douglas wrote this narrative, and yet I argue that she came to believe there is something fundamentally false, unrealistic, something too prescriptive, too simple, too pat, about it—at least as a solution to Cornelia's longtime, all-encompassing ignorance.

Unlike Connell's Mrs. Bridge who remains obstinately vapid and helpless to the end—she is (in the novel's final chapter) trapped in her Lincoln, whose engine had died, "halfway out of the garage . . . in such a position that the car doors were prevented from opening on one side by the garage petition, and on the other side by the wall"—Mrs. O'Kelly does indeed experience an awakening—of sorts. In chapter five, Jacobsen points out, "Cornelia seems to have broken free from her role as silent southern 'lady' and has found the strength to begin a new life on her own." An eloquent and accurate remark. Still, Cornelia's awakening is almost entirely ill-founded—it arises, specifically, out of two fantasies working in tandem: one, she imagines that Tweet is talking to her, guiding her through the city and through her grief; and two, she imagines that she has exhumed something from her past, that she has freed herself from the shackles of a long-ago secret. Cornelia's emotions do not, indeed *cannot*, correspond at all to reality; it seems quite reasonable to assume that Cornelia, so "adept at creating imaginary people and imaginary lives," experiences in New York City what might be called a *false epiphany*.

Douglas is aware of this, too. Indeed, chapter five—wherein the series of aforementioned events progress orchestrally toward this false epiphany, this intentional turn (as well as a *turning back*) in Cornelia's consciousness—is the most considered and intricate of the novel. When Cornelia and "Lewis" stand together at the apartment window watching the snow, James Joyce is invoked: the two alternately recite the opening sentences of the magnificent final paragraph of "The Dead"—"snow was general all over Ireland. It was falling on every part of the dark central plain, on the treeless hills, on the Bog of Allen," and so on—until, that is, he shushes her and they embrace. (An echo of Joyce's famous passage appears, too, almost forty pages earlier: "It's beginning to snow.

All last night and all today snow has been moving eastward across the country.") To insert Joyce into the moment in which Cornelia becomes, regardless of consequence or delusion, a person of action, a participant of the world, is to temper an otherwise cloyingly sentimental scene with parody. After all, Joyce brought "epiphany," a spiritual term, into the domain and parlance of literature. Therefore, behind the superficial romance of the scene, Douglas has tipped her cards in our direction, revealing that Cornelia and "Lewis" are in fact characters behaving as they must behave, as she needs them to behave. The tale-teller might have entered at this moment and attempted, say, to justify this tryst; instead, Douglas discovers a subtler option, as indeed the entire chapter (by continually referring to other art) has been working toward all along. She shows us that an artist can also be an artificer.

The narrator "falsifies" the epiphany, moreover, before it even occurs. She knows that something significant, particularly after Cornelia's Wordsworthian resignation in the willow leaves, must occur here in New York, but she believes that the all too frequent option of suicide (Edna Pontellier, Lily Bart, Emma Bovary, et al) didn't feel appropriate: "It's not in your character to kill yourself in this strange city." Once again like Mrs. Bridge, who could no more kill herself than she could escape her Lincoln, Cornelia is not, at least at this point in *Can't Quit You, Baby*, a woman of action. More practically, though, this would have ended the novel prematurely, would have left Tweet's narrative thread dangling. Douglas realizes that she has to get Cornelia back to Mississippi, back to Tweet, with some kind of narrative momentum or purpose, that the two women's stories must now overlap. In short, Cornelia cannot experience an authentic epiphany in the presence of a narrator who denies one course of action in order to admit another. Douglas is telling us that Cornelia's awakening, such as it is, is an authorial decision, not an experiential or introspective discovery made by Cornelia herself. A predetermined epiphany is inherently false.

Yet this false epiphany is extraordinarily effective. The narrator's very presence—"*I* am here, too, I, the tale-teller, to warn you, as I have before, that I have a stake in the story"—reveals the novel as artifice. Nevertheless, one of the primary ways in which an artist can obliterate artifice—"illusion"—is to paradoxically reveal the artifice of his or her art, seeing as it so often (and this is the case for *Can't Quit You, Baby*) implicates the artist him- or herself. Douglas makes the meta-narrator, the almost but not quite omniscient tale-teller, herself a tertiary character: "It is not only of Cornelia and Tweet that one must say: Your lives have become so entangled that you can never separate them. Not of them only." In this way, Douglas is able to maintain the reader's interest in the narrative of these women's struggle, even as she openly denies their autonomy—an attribute so crucial to the illusion of realist mimetic fiction. Put another way, because she has just obliterated the illusion that Cornelia makes her own decisions, Douglas brings the tale-teller to the fore: without eclipsing the storyline or usurping Cornelia's role as protagonist, the tale-teller now becomes the "realist" character who thinks and acts autonomously.

But of course Cornelia and Tweet's lives are not truly "entangled," as the tale-teller states above, but are merely entangled in the mind of Cornelia (who suddenly hears "Tweet's voice") and of the tale-teller herself (who has undertaken the project of entangling them in the first place). The idea of entangling seems to arise from René Magritte's *L'Assassin Menace* (*The Menaced Assassin*) (1927), the painting Cornelia studies at the MOMA, and Ingmar Bergman's *Persona* (1966), the film she watches in New York and which also, incidentally, announces itself as an artifice, a filmic construction, from its famous opening sequence: a series of images of camera equipment, projectors, lights, darkness, and provocative photographs (e.g. an erect penis). Though it's never mentioned by its title in the novel, the film is by its very description indisputably *Persona*. Let us first discuss the film, summarized thus by the tale-teller: "And now this movie that Cornelia has just seen, in which an actress who has not spoken for six months is cared for by a young, unsophisticated, chattering nurse, a movie in which the two women, alone together in a house by the sea, seem slowly to take on each other's personalities, characters, lives, even come to look alike." By turns frighteningly honest and frighteningly cruel, Alma and Elisabet in *Persona* have an entangled and complicated relationship indeed, and the film entangles Cornelia and Tweet further, at least in Cornelia's head.

Importantly, Cornelia was essentially without a voice in the opening chapters of the novel, seeing as she responded to Tweet's fluency only occasionally and then with put-on displays of prudish shock or stuck-up virtue: "It's a waste of time and energy to hate people, Cornelia said. I don't hate anybody." She seems to believe that Tweet's inability to speak is akin to Elisabet's decision not to, as well as to her own previous inability to speak (and act) authentically. (Alma's sexual escapade might have more easily convinced Cornelia to sleep with "Lewis," too.) Back in Mississippi, playing Alma to Tweet's Elizabet, Cornelia takes Tweet's hand: "I know you're in there, she said. How can we persuade you to come out?" This is one of the most cringe-worthy moments of the novel: Cornelia, having adopted yet another fantasy, that of a nurse, doesn't understand that no amount of *persuasion* can make Tweet talk. The woman has an aneurysm—"A bubble," Rosa tells Cornelia. "A *bubble!* Say it might be getting bigger in there, squeezing everything up. Might bust"—and she simply needs to undergo the hard work of recovery, as indeed she does. In short, these women's lives are, even at this late stage in the novel, not truly entangled at all; they are merely entangled in Cornelia's imagination and in, of course, the tale-teller's decision to tell a tale about them. Like the figures in Magritte's *L'Assassin Menace*, the three of them are framed together in separate, isolated spaces.

Douglas in fact tips her hat to this faux entanglement when Cornelia, right before seeing *Persona*, happens across Magritte's painting in the Museum of Modern Art. The work might be described as a triptych by depth: in the foreground, on either side of the painting's central room, stand two waiting men, one with a club, one with a net; in the middle ground, a woman lies naked on a sofa, bleeding from the mouth, most likely dead, and a man (possibly her killer) stands before the horn of an old Victrola, casual, perhaps meditative, his right hand in his pocket; and in the background, three men peek over the bottom of a window—only their heads are visible—into the central room. The implicit narrative here, if there is one, seems to matter less than the spatial relationship of the figures. Three pages later, when Cornelia is staring out of a bus window, the tale-teller says: "[T]hose mysterious figures in the painting, so closely, so intimately joined, one dead, one about to die, two about to become killers, three witnesses—all of whose lives and deaths, no matter that no one knows why, must be entangled beyond extricating." The most significant feature of this painting in relation to Douglas's novel is, as Matthew Luter states, "it depicts several separate physical spaces within one canvas, all of which are occupied by multiple characters, none of whom can see everyone else in the painting." And yet they exist together, are trapped together, in artful composition, for our viewing pleasure or confusion or investigation. Likewise, Cornelia and Tweet (and to a lesser extent everyone else, such as Tweet's husband and Cornelia's children) are incapable of seeing one another; each exists in separate physical and/or psychic spaces altogether; even when they're in the kitchen together, for instance, Cornelia's abstention from reality—she just turns off, or significantly lowers the volume of, her hearing aid—prevents any human connection at all. Nevertheless, all are undoubtedly entangled in Douglas's novel, and naturally, therefore, in readers' minds.

Still, why entangle them in this particular way? In my view, Douglas is interrogating the potentiality and limitations of art, the often chasm-like separation of art and life. In some sense, Cornelia becomes in this fifth chapter a surrogate Ellen Douglas; after all, she, in writing this novel, is—like

Cornelia—merely imagining Tweet's voice, as opposed to truly hearing it, truly being spoken to: she's trying to use art and the imagination to improve, however obliquely, racial conflict; she's trying to intersect the consciousnesses of these two women, to entangle their *spirits* (so to speak), to forge a connection beyond or deeper than the body. (Alma to Elisabet: "Is it possible to be one and the same person at the same time? I mean, two people?") Failure or no, the novel attempts to push back against Auden's oft-quoted line (from "In Memory of W.B. Yeats"): "poetry"—and I think we might say *fiction*, too—"makes nothing happen."

Significantly, moreover, Cornelia and Tweet belong to very different socioeconomic classes. Cornelia can escape to New York for a weekend, visit the MOMA, catch a Bergman film—she is capable, in other words, of participating as a spectator in the bourgeois tradition of European art—whereas travel and art are, for Tweet, not merely indulgences but in fact impossibilities: "[Tweet] is poor. The measure of her poverty is that she considers Cornelia (who thinks of herself as modestly well-off) immensely wealthy."[4] In contrast to this somewhat elitist tradition, Tweet's art—the blues—is a folk art, a public art, an art of the people, particularly of the disenfranchised, the disinherited, the down-and-out. More specifically, as Robert Rea writes, "the blues and blues lyrics contain essentialized fragments of African American life." Just as Tweet's voice, appropriated or not, is essential to the novel's aim to cross racial boundaries, so must Tweet's art be represented. Though *Can't Quit You, Baby* does not attempt to create a hierarchy of art or of artistic traditions, Douglas clearly reveals that art is not immune to class distinctions/barriers and that artistic traditions are indeed features of society that necessarily, even if inadvertently, include and exclude. What, after all, could be further from Tweet's consciousness than a Magritte painting? Her concerns are inescapably more practical, more fundamental—a role the blues itself holds in the context of American music. As Willie Dixon said countless times (an axiom for him and many other bluesmen and -women): "The blues are the roots and the other musics are the fruits." Or as the bassist and bandleader Creole, from James Baldwin's "Sonny's Blues," says wordlessly with his music:

> [The blues] were not about anything very new. He and his boys up there were keeping it new, at the risk of ruin, destruction, madness, and death, in order to find new ways to make us listen. For, while the tale of how we suffer, and how we are delighted, and how we may triumph is never new, it always must be heard. There isn't any other tale to tell, it's the only light we've got in all this darkness.

Therefore Douglas, a white southern woman, savvy to the bourgeois traditions of Western European art (literature, painting, cinema, etc), realizes that the goal of the novel—to write a realist mimetic narrative that transcends racism—however noble or decent, can never be accomplished, and not only because she can't truly speak for or about any disenfranchised group but because the very means by which she "speaks" (that is to say, *the novel itself*) is virtual and impractical, a bourgeois indulgence. As Douglas herself states in her wonderful essay "Writing and Reality": "The real world is flesh and blood and steel and wind and smoke and tears and dirt and stones and water. A story is words on paper, an emotional and intellectual structure made of language and meant to express meaning." In "A Defence of Poetry," Shelley said famously that poets—and again we might include *fiction writers* or *novelists* here—are the "unacknowledged legislators of the world," to which Douglas might reply: "Yes. Exactly. And what effect can an *unacknowledged legislator* have on the world, anyway?" There are limitations to art and to the imagination, even though our tale-teller "begins, as every storyteller does, with the illusion of freedom."

The first four chapters of the novel alternate perspectives like a failed call and response; that is to say, the chapters simply exist side by side. Whereas Tweet narrates her chapters (1 and 3) to an unresponsive, barely listening Cornelia, Cornelia's chapters (2 and 4) don't even incorporate Tweet at all until chapter 5, and then, as mentioned above, it's merely an imagined Tweet.[5] The novel's sixth and final chapter, then, which at last contains the two women together, in the flesh, trying to communicate with one another, seems primed (despite the tale-teller's authorial struggles) for reconciliation, unity, acceptance. Importantly, Douglas doesn't alter the structure of her novel in response to the tale-teller's gnawing trepidation and insufficiency: "Can't someone else search for the end of this story? Discover where it is leading us?" Quite to the contrary—and this is an ingenious move—the tale-teller delivers the very novel, remains well within the very conventions, that she has been interrogating and resisting from the beginning, though the reader, having experienced a false epiphany, having seen that the narrative is an artifice, is now skeptical, suspicious. After a brief, vicious outburst of anger from both sides, Cornelia and Tweet find themselves "on the floor together, picking up the strings of beads, the plastic doubloons," that had fallen during their argument, and the two women just as quickly make up, begin to laugh, and are at the very end of the book—when Tweet begins to sing to Cornelia from her front porch: "I love you, darlin, but I hate your treacherous low down ways"—on the cusp of an actual call and response. Then, after a section break, the tale-teller concludes the novel with the following imperatives: "Sing it, Tweet. Yeah. Sing it, Cornelia. Sing it." Thus ends Douglas's novel of racial reconciliation. Cornelia and Tweet are at long last, under the direction of the tale-teller, singing to and for one another. Or are they? First fight, then laugh, then sing—is it, perhaps, too easy an equation?

These final sentences strike me as intentionally ambiguous and sentimental. Are Tweet and Cornelia singing together at the end of the book? Are they merely being told to sing? Is the tale-teller's voice sounding in readers' heads, just as Tweet's voice sounded in Cornelia's in New York City, so that we readers become not only co-creators of the novel's ending but also, implicitly, of the future at large? Let's parse this out. We know that Tweet sings from her porch; even so, we also know that Cornelia doesn't sing in the text at all—even if, to be fair, she doesn't have the opportunity to sing; a section break may have cut her off. In all likelihood, however, Douglas wanted readers to feel that Cornelia and Tweet were indeed singing together, or at last emotionally capable of singing together; wanted us to feel the silence of the page from which, someday, music might issue—an as-yet-inaudible duet charged with potentiality. As Jacobsen has written: "Tweet's song…suggests that there is room for an alternative discourse between the two women—a space where authentic friendship can develop." Yet we must remember the artificiality of the novel; we must remember the false epiphany in New York, the almost cloying sentimentality that, in addition to the presence of Joyce's "The Dead," marked it as parody: "I'd sing you a song if I could sing, he said early in the morning before he went away. / I think you did, she said." Furthermore, after Tweet sings a few lines of a song from her porch, she calls out to Cornelia, "That's how the song goes"—a comment resistant to pat resolution, as though she's saying, "This is how things are and may always be" (i.e. I may continue to love you, but I may also continue to hate your treacherous low down ways). In short, given the previous false epiphany and the metafictive interrogations employed throughout, the subtle ambiguity and blatant sentimentality of the novel's ending forces the reader to suspect the sincerity as well as the likelihood of such a facile reconciliation.

And yet the great guileful triumph of this novel is that, despite its postmodern strategies (the false epiphany, "the illusion of freedom," the metafictive musings and interrogations, the variety of storytelling styles, the polyvocality, etc), the book's desire to be a traditional realist narrative that takes an optimistic stance on race relations is so strong that the aforementioned skepticism and suspicion—that is to say, Douglas's ability to recognize that she is in fact insufficient to her art's demands—all of these qualities actually buttress the unwarranted, perhaps naïve, stance of a brighter future. Put another way, idealism and skepticism exist side by side, and the skepticism paradoxically strengthens the idealism. Just as Douglas exposes the artifice of the novel in order make a more authentic text, so the tale-teller interrogates her own telling in order to make more authentic, more nuanced, and more persuasive the idealistic impulse out of which the story initially arose. Thus the novel's title takes on another meaning, too: not only can Tweet and Cornelia not quit each other, but the tale-teller can't quit them either. (A stark contrast to Billie Holiday's lyric in "Long Gone Blues": "Are you trying to quit me, baby, but you don't know how.") The novel's title highlights Douglas's stubborn and courageous clinging to the novel's original idealistic impulse.

To understand the effectiveness of this conclusion, I think it's useful to compare it to the conclusion of other novels that attempt, even if very differently, to narratively reconcile race relations. Take, for example, Bernard Malamud's *The Tenants*, a novel in which Jewish American writer Harry Lesser and African American writer William Spearmint (pennamed Bill Spear), by turns writerly companions and sworn enemies, are the sole tenants of a soon-to-be-torn-down apartment building. To conclude his novel, Malamud takes the opposite approach to Douglas: *The Tenants* concludes not with a sentimental, idealistic song—"I love you, baby, but I hate your treacherous low down ways"—but rather with a desperate, pleading, over-the-top anti-song: Levenspeil, landlord of the apartment building and, in this scene, surrogate reader, cries out "mercy" one-hundred-and-thirteen times (I counted) without punctuation. For me, this renders Harry and Bill's ultra-violent power struggles—by novel's end, Harry has split Willie's skull with an axe at the same moment Willie castrates Harry with a knife—utterly ridiculous. Here, as critic Edmund Spevack states in his essay "Racial Conflict and Multiculturalism: Bernard Malamud's *The Tenants*": "communication and cooperation between races, cultural individualities, and...divergent conceptions of literature has finally failed." Importantly, the reader, suspicious of the likelihood of either novel's conclusion, nevertheless yearns for the conclusion of *Can't Quit You, Baby*, and outright rejects the shameless, absurd, repulsive, violent conclusion of *The Tenants*. It's important to note that these two novels felt the need to separate themselves in the end from reality, from the status quo, so that the reader might return to reality with a difference, might become, for instance, more aware or sensitive or compassionate.

Beside *The Tenants*, whose realism disintegrates into nightmare, *Can't Quit You, Baby* sacrifices realism in order to present a world that is better than our world—to set in motion the "journey toward a more vast reality," to borrow a phrase from James Baldwin—however sentimental or naïve or dreamily soft-edged it may appear to readers, or even to Douglas herself. Indeed, beside *The Tenants*, Douglas is a diehard optimist: despite the tale-teller's continuous interrogations, she will not allow her own novelistic failures to disillusion her, to make her turn her back on hope. Like Halberstam's "queer art of failure," Douglas's novel "turns on the impossible, the improbable, the unlikely, and the unremarkable. It quietly loses, and in losing it imagines other goals for life, for love, for art, and for being."

Ultimately, *Can't Quit You, Baby* employs a variety of realist and postmodern strategies to craftily and ethically present a novel capable of transcending racial barriers, and I have tried here to illuminate the ways in which Douglas and her tale-teller struggle with and against both the telling and the impulse and authority to tell such a story in the first place, focusing largely on the novel's constellation of allusions (Wordsworth, Joyce, Bergman, Magritte), its disclosure of itself as an artifice, and the subsequent false epiphany that at once forces Cornelia and Tweet to more humane interaction. I believe we can also more readily admire the subtle and artful ways in which Douglas necessarily fails yet, to invoke Beckett, *fails better*: the technical skill and stylistic range (Tweet's oral storytelling, Cornelia's interior fantasies, a fairy tale, a parody, and so on) required to write a novel as prismatic and guileful as *Can't Quit You, Baby* is astounding—all of it held together in a delicate, web-like balance. I can think of no other novel that is so modestly ambitious: short but intense; cunning yet straightforward; equally engaged with art and life, with writing and reality; political without being didactic; referential without being erudite. *Can't Quit You, Baby* is indeed an incredible testament of aesthetic and humanitarian integration.

NOTES

1. More specifically, in the penultimate and antepenultimate paragraphs of this essay, I discuss the contradistinctive ways in which Douglas and Malamud abandon realism in the final scenes of their respective novels, not only to unveil a precedent for such a "move"—*The Tenants* appeared sixteen years before *Can't Quit You, Baby*—but also to highlight, in stark contrast to Malamud's bloody climax, Douglas's unflinching, if naïve, optimism.

2. Douglas also retold classic fairy tales in *The Magic Carpet* (1987), as well as created fairybook characters like the Toad—a "smarmy, horrifying, idiotic, doting" neighbor who is "so short she can walk under the dining-room table without bending her head"—in *A Lifetime Burning* (1982) and the monstrous Howie Snyder ("skin glowing green under the lamp on the desk . . . claws! green powerful claws of a dinosaur") in *Apostles of Light* (1973).

3. I mean "coming back" not only psychologically ("The human heart dares not stay away too long from that which hurt it most," wrote Lillian Smith) but physically, too: Cornelia's interlude in New York is a laughably miniature bildungsroman, a motif common among southern writers and their writing (Richard Wright in Chicago; Faulkner's Quentin Compson in Cambridge, Mass.; Ernest J. Gaines in San Francisco; and the lesser-known Alan McLaurin, poet-narrator of Douglas's own 1979 novel *The Rock Cried Out*: "[B]y November I had begun to feel a pull—like gravity,

maybe, whatever it is that makes one sure the world is the best planet we have and that one's own part of it is a necessary spiritual terrain, as much one's own as a cast in the eye—that drew me southward again").

4. It's also important to note that, post-chapter five, Tweet can no longer successfully carry a chapter in her own voice, anyway: the reader has become all too aware that even Tweet's realistic voice exists within a human-made artifact (i.e. the novel itself).

5. I recall the socioeconomic disparity in Reuben Jackson's comic poem "sunday brunch":

>and where
>do your parents
>summer?
>she asked
>him.
>
>the front porch,
>he replied.

Think Vertically!

NOTES FROM A COMP TEACHER'S DIARY

To write well, one must first allow oneself to write poorly.

*

I try to create in my classroom an encouraging and accepting environment—a space of non-judgment—in which student writers are not merely permitted but in fact *goaded* to fail and to feel unashamed of their mistakes.

*

Ornette Coleman: "There's no such thing as bad music, only bad performances."

*

My pedagogy is built quite simply upon encouragement, enthusiasm, investment, participation, and generosity.

*

My assignments aim to establish in my students the daily habit or rhythm of ingesting and producing texts, the way some people meditate or shoot free throws or practice the bassoon.

*

The only way to improve one's writing is to read and write . . . a lot. So my students read and write . . . a lot.

*

Miles attributed the majority of his growth as a musician to the New York clubs and to his experience alongside Charlie Parker. Writers are luckier in this regard: our Birdland is the local library.

*

For years, Michael Ondaatje worked on a rolling poem called "Elimination Dance," a seemingly endless litany of peculiar descriptions: "those who have pissed out of the back of moving trucks," "those who have woken to find the wet footprint of a peacock across their kitchen floor," "those who, after a swim, find the sensation of water dribbling out of their ears erotic," and so on.

*

For writers, the words THE END are never the end.

*

Poets like Brenda Hillman and David St. John often deny resolution by "ending" with em dashes or ellipses . . .

*

Kristen Case: "[Emily] Dickinson held off periods like the little deaths they are."

*

I used to have my students reflect, journal-style, on their essays. But most of them believed that those reflections were extraneous and that their essays were the "real" writing. Making no such distinction myself, I now create exercises that fuse reflection and essay writing: Write reflective paragraphs between each paragraph of your essay, for example. I don't care if they cut these paragraphs later; after all, one can write paragraphs between paragraphs (reflective or not) ad infinitum. I simply want to see them reflect, the way a math teacher requires them to "show their work."

*

Frank Bidart: "Making is the mirror in which we see ourselves."

*

I once played alongside an extraordinary Indian-born tenor saxophonist. Between sets, I asked him how he had learned to so easily stretch the boundaries of a given key. He lit a Pall Mall, shook out the match, and advised me to play the sitar — that is to say, to play with quartertones, with microtones. "There are always notes," he told me, "between the notes."

*

An example of Zeno's paradox: one can write toward a subject and still never, as it were, touch it.

*

In any event, if taken seriously, my students' reflective paragraphs are almost always the most interesting for the reader and the most useful for the writer.

*

Just as a music critic's understanding of Bach's Cello Suites are deepened by learning how to play the cello, or a car enthusiast's understanding of cars is made more nuanced by restoring a clunker, so learning how texts are made (or trying to learn, anyway) will no doubt enhance one's understanding of them.

*

In my early twenties, I typed out Cormac McCarthy's *Child of God* (1973) on my laptop. I just loved (and still love) the relentless tap-shoe percussion of computer keys. More importantly, though, it was instructive to see a typeset novel on 8.5 x 11 sheets of paper: the McCarthy paragraphs I was emulating in my own writing were, I realized, about twice as long as McCarthy's.

*

Student writers should not shy away from imitation. As Clark Terry, the great jazz trumpeter, once said: "There's nothing wrong with being a copycat, so long as you copy the right cats." Indeed, imitation may be—paradoxically—one of the surest ways to develop one's voice: one cannot *not* be oneself.

*

A few years ago, after a night of sipping 12-year-old Glenfiddich, my friend Alan remarked: "I like you when you're drunk. You're just, well, more *Jaydn*."

*

I believe a classroom of student writers can be a perpetual motion machine—it can run on its collective energy. Workshops and peer reviews and sharing sessions, in which students carry on semester-long conversations about and within their work, are at the very heart of this energy.

*

Robert Creeley: "Poetry is a team sport."

*

The ultimate goal of any teacher is to make him- or herself wholly unnecessary. Hence, the best writing teachers, having nothing better to do, write alongside their students.

*

All writing is creative—even in-class exercises, even a cover letter, even a diary entry.

*

Alex Katz, one of my favorite painters, tells a story of visiting a friend's studio in (if memory serves) the Bronx. This was the 50s. Existentialism was all the rage. Katz says he looked around, spotted a book by Camus on his friend's coffee table, and thought: "Oh, for Christ's sake, can't we just have a good time!"

*

Reading and writing should be taught as pleasures.

*

Young writers tend to make frequent and bold declarations about writing, then frequently and boldly denounce them.

*

Flexibility is so important for us. My students and I will often rewrite a great sentence by, say, James Baldwin—"On the morning of the third of August, we drove my father to the graveyard through a wilderness of smashed plate glass" ("Notes to a Native Son")—over and over again, rearranging clauses, injecting our own descriptions or metaphors, swapping out Baldwin's words for our own words, etc. One can express a single thought in a gazillion ways.

*

No "way" is better than any other, either. In writing, objectivity does not exist. I like to begin my courses by listening to Caroline Bergvall read her conceptual poem "VIA"—a gathering of 48 translations of the opening sentence to Dante's *Inferno*. Afterward, I ask my students which translation is the strongest, which is the clearest, which is the most memorable, and so on, but of course they cannot reach a consensus. Not even close.

*

I expose my students to a variety of styles and subjects, techniques and mannerisms, philosophies and imaginations. In literature as in genetics, diversity flourishes.

*

I sometimes suggest they change their compositional units, which will of course change the way they think. Essayists think in arguments. Novelists think in scenes. Poets think in lines. Haikuists think in syllables. Stephen King thinks in deadlines.

*

One of my primary goals is to protect the student writer from the influence or supremacy of any one literary aesthetic or cultural representation.

*

A decade ago, at a diner, my father asked our waitress what kind of juice they served. He'd jogged several miles to meet me there and now sat in the booth, sweating through his tank top and Speedo shorts. The waitress listed the juices: apple, orange, cranberry, grapefruit—. "I'll have that," he interrupted. "Which one?" she asked. "All of 'em. One of each," he said.

*

Marvin Bell: "Originality is just a new amalgam of influences."

*

Late one night, when one of his seventeen-odd harpsichord-playing sons stopped on the seventh note of a major scale, J.S. Bach famously stormed downstairs, banged the tonic, then turned right around and went back to bed—unable to sleep, legend has it, until the scale had been resolved.

*

Monterey Jazz Festival, 1965. Dizzy Gillespie begins to tune his horn to the piano but stops prematurely. He leans into the mic and says huskily: "That's close enough for jazz."

*

Wittgenstein: "The limits of your language are the limits of your world."

*

I therefore resist teaching "rules," even basic grammar rules. After all, our best writers are like Neo in *The Matrix*—to him or her, the rules simply do not apply.

*

"I believe in ending sentences with a preposition," said Heather Christle, "in order to give the ideas a way out."

*

Last night, my friend and fellow writer d. sent me a series of text messages: *as teachers, we are always correcting students.* And a minute later: *what we call a mistake or error may be a moment of transition on a path to something new.* And a few minutes later still: *we deny the very possibility of transition and of newness.*

*

d. writes in all lowercase because, he says, it is humbler.

*

Yet I sometimes will make suggestions. When beginning an essay, for example, I suggest my students aim somewhere between these two opposing (and equally laughable) dictums: Ginsberg's "First thought, best thought," and Coleridge's "Best words, best order." Put simply, I believe revision improves writing and that perfection is a chimera.

*

In middle school, when I was learning how to solo on the electric bass, my father would sometimes holler from a distant room: "Think vertically!"

*

As a boy, Salvador Dali had difficulty learning how to read because he was so engrossed in the shapes of the letters.

*

Phillip Lopate: "Tilt your limitations away from the viewer."

*

"Quote widely, quote often," the poet Stephen Kuusisto once advised me.

*

Though he couldn't read music, my blind bass teacher, Mike Kelly, had the most astonishing ear—an ear that exceeded perfect pitch, an ear that actually anticipated my every move/instinct. I understood early that, if I was going to please anybody, I had to surprise 'em.

*

Constraints, then, which incite the unexpected, are not merely for the poets. Last week, I made my students write a three-paragraph in-class essay about their first semester in college; they had to incorporate the words *flower, rage, tumultuous, sweat, facilitated, speedboat*. One student wrote: "Life is a tumultuous ocean, and I'm driving the speedboat of knowledge, sweaty with rage."

*

"A writer is not so much someone who has something to say," said William Stafford, "as he is someone who has found a process that will bring about new things he would not have thought of if he had not started to say them."

*

I once told the poet Joseph Millar that my recent writing lacked intensity. He told me to write with a knife in one hand.

*

As a jazz musician, many of my writing exercises attempt to incorporate improvisation—the part of the grade-conscious student's mind that acts first and thinks later.

*

Somebody despises every text. A number of intelligent people believe Shakespeare should be forgotten. "Get used to it," I tell my students. "Learn to accept criticism as a perpetual symptom of writing. Indeed, learn to embrace it."

> [H]e had done as he liked, he had gone his own way, built his castle in the air. And if in the end he had dreamed the wrong dream, the dream that others didn't wish to enter, then that was the way of dreams, it was only to be expected, he had no desire to have dreamt otherwise.
>
> —Steven Millhauser's *Martin Dressler* (1996)

*

Writers should take any criticism—especially a teacher's or a critic's—with the proverbial grain of salt.

*

Like the bedroom, the page is a small private arena in which to experiment, in which to explore oneself and others.

*

Each writer must develop his or her own process(es), which is why Kent Haruf writes in his basement with a black sack over his head.

*

Was that also why the fabulous *New Yorker* cartoonist Saul Steinberg used to hide his daughter's name, Nina, in each of his cartoons?

*

In preparation for a Q-&-A, John Cage asked himself questions and memorized his answers. On the day of the event, when the audience asked their own questions, Cage simply rattled off the answers he had memorized, forcing the audience to make connections between unconnected ideas.

*

Dr. Rick Shubert, my first philosophy professor, once told me that the answer to a Zen koan would be, if one grasped the thousand-linked chain of their logical connection, a mere truism.

*

Dr. Johnson defined a net as "a lot of holes held together by a string."

*

Birch trees, continental quilt, tulip glass, prose poetry, Denver omelet, my heart.

*

It pains me to talk so frequently about student theses, to reduce the trajectories and topographies and idiosyncrasies of their texts to single sentences. I feel we've either dropped anchor before the adventure's even begun or—worse—summed up an entire life with a pithy phrase.

*

Anyway, in paradise, every sentence is a thesis.

*

When I fall in love with a writer, I attempt to read everything he or she has written. David Shapiro, when asked which Frank O'Hara poem was the best, replied: "His *Collected Poems*."

*

This morning my daughter and I spent forty minutes trying to fit a circular block into a square hole. Writing is not so much difficult as it is a time-consuming test of perseverance.

*

"There's a pale romance to the watchmaker God . . ." wrote Robert Lowell. "He loved to tinker."

*

Sometimes, with enough patience and luck, the circle fits perfectly into the square.

*

I want the classroom to be, in bell hooks' words, "the most radical space of possibility in the academy."

*

The intimate subjectivity of writing, combined with its aspiration toward generality (in order to communicate widely), has always made me feel, as a reader, less alone in the world—a fact perhaps especially true for practitioners, in whom literature holds a dearer and more central role.

The teaching of writing is a deeply significant, deeply rewarding act of reciprocation and community.

*

I teach because I had incredible teachers and because I have incredible students.

*

Marcel Duchamp: "I don't believe in art. I believe in artists."

*

Or, more reasonably, I think: *First the artist, then the art.*

In Praise of Constraints

INCITING THE UNEXPECTED

Language is a box you wear over your head.
—Nona Caspers

Several years ago, I began to write poems whose lines were of uniform length. I must admit that, in the beginning, this constraint constituted a poetic manifestation of obsessive-compulsive disorder: I loved the way a poem composed of conventional spacing could, without resorting to justified margins, resemble a near-perfect rectangle. But I also loved the contrast between the subjectivity of a poem and its objective appearance on the page. Even though most of my early attempts suffered as a result of this constraint—I often sacrificed words and images for the sake of satisfying a line-length—I continued to write these "rectangles" obsessively. Then, after a month or so, I began to notice that, when I was stubborn enough, when I had worked a line until I was pleased both with its length and its poetic value, this constraint was a reliable way in which to incite arresting, largely unexpected results. Like established formal constraints (rhyme, meter, syllabics, etc), an arbitrary, uniform line-length could, I discovered, force a poet to go beyond normative language and familiar sensory experience. I was forced to explore the possibilities of a given line, and this often meant radically altering—not simply expanding or contracting—the language. Just as a line of Creeley's will, with his emphasis on the breath, "say as much as it can, or as little, in the 'time' given," so a line of mine attempts to say as much as it can, or as little, in the *space* given.

This is slow, often tedious work. I wrote well over 10,000 words before I placed the final period on a recent 164-word poem entitled "Ritornello (or, Landscape with X)." Worlds apart, in short, from Ginsberg's famous dictum: "First thought, best thought." Still, I very much enjoy my strange, idiosyncratic constraint: it is an engaging game; there's nothing static about it. Indeed, my experiences trying to "find" lines of particular lengths have inadvertently become some of the most surprising and affecting of my poetry-writing life.

Importantly, though writing poetry can be a mental, emotional, and imaginative workout, to write with constraints is not simply to use and abuse a certain set of muscles; it is also to discover fresh, inventive ways in which to compensate for what's lacking, for the proverbial arm tied behind one's back. Despite the general slowness of the process—or perhaps precisely *because* of its slowness—the trick is to keep moving, to trust that movement in due course will end in discovery. Or else to trust that movement is itself the discovery. The parallels with trends in twentieth-century art, particularly Abstract Expressionism, are striking. "At a certain moment the canvas began to appear to one American painter after another as an arena in which to act," wrote art critic Harold Rosenberg. And this, for me, for my rectangles—a canvas inside the larger canvas of the page—is generally the case. I write a lot and I discard a lot, but deletion is as active and as productive a gesture as writing itself. I simply keep moving. Keep moving . . .

Now, years later, continuing to work with rectangles, I have come to care less about the appearance of the poems—that is, line-length uniformity—than the unexpected results this constraint incites. "A writer is not so much someone who has something to say," said William Stafford, "as he is someone who has found a process that will bring about new things he would not have thought of if he had not started to say them." In fact, I have come to rely upon this process as a means of igniting my imagination, of "inviting the muse," of digging deeper, of losing and discovering (in semi-equal measure) the self. I suppose I am, in Denise Levertov's words, "as enamored of the process of making as of the thing made." This essay will examine how certain other contemporary poets—truong tran, Christian Bök, Charles Wright (briefly), and Harryette Mullen—have imposed a variety of similar, seemingly arbitrary constraints to alter, in a variety of unexpected ways, their own poetry.

*

Because a constraint can, relative to its invasiveness or its level of difficulty, moderately or radically alter a poem, it's fruitful to look at some book-length constraints—or, at least, some individual poems within those books—to appreciate the spectrum of alteration that's not only possible but also sustainable. Let us begin with a fairly moderate example: truong tran's *four letter words* (2008), a collection of mostly unpunctuated, uncapitalized, untitled prose poems, which he calls "bricks."

this poem the line every single word the slanted rhyme the image the red bird the boy the color grey the space in between the words the letters wondering the wanderings the illusion of a brick this book the title its reflection in the mirror the page the act of turning turning back the tide the apple the core this poem is everything the box the poem a lie written a lie in response if the you fictitious are looking for look in the folds where paper meets spine where the edge is contained where nowhere is a place to look to go look just beyond the last line written look in between that space in between

To omit punctuation is to omit sentences and clauses; and yet, because our mind tends to organize, tran's poems remain quite readable. To omit punctuation, however, is also to allow for chance error—"chance to break the spell of our habitual literary expectations and to approach the condition of what has been called 'free imagination,'" as Charles Simic wrote in "Negative Capability and Its Children." tran is allowing, in other words, for multiple, unintended meanings. Consider this (from tran's *four letter words*): "boyish he responds to the boy baffled i've been in exile the word is my house imprisoned as if it is at the edge," which can be read, if punctuated, a number of different ways: "boyish, he responds to the boy, baffled: 'i've been in exile.' the word is my house, imprisoned, as if it is at the edge"; or, "boyish, he responds to the boy. baffled i've been. in exile, the word is my house, imprisoned, as if it is at the edge"; or—but the point is clear enough. The word-arrangement of tran's poem is in a sense prismatic, since so many "implied sentences" exist simultaneously. By omitting all punctuation, as well as all line- and stanza-breaks—again: a fairly moderate constraint—tran is able to break away from some significant literary expectations and to produce, as a result, a more startling, multidimensional poetry.

> indulge me this one time and try something new not really new but strange to the skin not really skin but language as skin

*

The most radical recent example of a book-length constraint, on the other hand, might be Christian Bök's *Eunoia* (2001), a book of lipograms, divided into five chapters (A, E, I, O, and U), in which every poem can contain any consonant but only its respective chapter's vowel. (Bök's constraint is, then, to exclude certain vowels.) *Eunoia* took Bök seven years to write—and people like to make a big deal about this—but seven years strikes me as not too much time at all, given that the constraint (to use only one vowel per poem) impacts every single word:

> Writing is inhibiting. Sighing, I sit, scribbling in ink this pidgin script. I sing with nihilistic witticism, disciplining signs with trifling gimmicks—impish hijinks which highlight stick sigils. Isn't it glib? Isn't it chic? I fit childish insights within rigid limits, writing shtick which might instill priggish misgivings in critics blind with hindsight. I dismiss nitpicking criticism which flirts with philistinism. I bitch; I kibitz—griping whilst criticizing dimwits, sniping whilst indicting nitwits, dismissing simplistic thinking, in which philippic wit is still illicit.

This can be, to be sure, maddening work. Like writing in a straitjacket. Nevertheless, it would be difficult to believe that such a difficult and invasive constraint would not incite—nay, necessitate—unexpected results. Indeed, in addition to creating compelling sounds ("Dutch smut churns up blushful succubus lusts"), the very intention of a lipogram is to incite strange new material. For this very reason, Bök is forced to adapt to the extreme language conditions that he himself has imposed, and he succeeds unequivocally: I can think of no stronger nor more radical example of language adaptation than Christian Bök's *Eunoia*.

Furthermore, though *Eunoia* might appear obdurately youthful, such extreme rebellion against linguistic norms is itself a form of expression, an aesthetic stance that rejects Wordsworth's claim that poetry is "the spontaneous overflow of powerful emotions recollected in tranquility." (Today, Bök's no longer writing "poems" at all, but rather encoding language into the DNA of *E. Coli*, hoping the language will be preserved for millions of years.) Poetry, for Bök, is a cryptographer's art: it's about discovering and expanding the possibilities of poetic expression. *Eunoia*'s renunciation of certain letters, which forecloses (in the act of composition) access to certain words and phrases and trains of thought, proves to be a most effective way in which to accomplish this.

*

Before moving on (*keep moving . . .*), I feel impelled to make two qualifying, if obvious, distinctions among constraints: all constraints are characterized by, one, their level of strictness and, two, their level of discernibility. A lipogram, an example of a very strict restraint, is what David Orr calls a "mechanical form." In his words, "A mechanical form involves a simple rule based on inclusion, exclusion, counting, or some similar procedure. . . . [M]echanical forms typically don't allow for the idea of degree: A lipogram that fails to obey its governing rule doesn't register as a 'loose' lipogram; it just seems like a mistake." I agree absolutely. Yet there are many poets who impose upon their writing more malleable or forgiving forms, which do indeed allow for the idea of degree. Consider, for example, the use of "dropped" lines in Charles Wright's *Sestets* (2009), a book of sixty-nine, six-line poems—his constraint being one of brevity, then—in which only left-flushed lines are counted as autonomous. That the dropped portion be considered part of the same line is, of course, a literary convention. Even so, the convention allows Wright to have his cake and eat it too: though he likely used dropped lines for a number of reasons—for emphasis, for look, for light, for air—he can nevertheless break a line and only count one of them among the six, as here:

TOMORROW

The metaphysics of the quotidian was what he was after:
A little dew on the sunrise grass,
A drop of blood in the evening trees,
                               a drop of fire.

If you don't shine you are darkness.
The future is merciless,

everyone's name inscribed
On the flyleaf of the Book of Snow.

But constraints can also be characterized by their level of discernibility. In general, the stricter the constraint, the easier it is to discern. We might compare, for instance, two poems from Harryette Mullen's *Sleeping with the Dictionary* (2002)—"Variations on a Theme Park" and "Dim Lady"—two corruptions of Shakespeare's Sonnet 130, a "Dark Lady" Sonnet. It's important to note that "Variation on a Theme Park" is an N+7, one of Oulipo's better-known creations—that is, a poem (based on an existing text) in which each substantive noun is replaced by the seventh noun following or sometimes preceding it in a dictionary. Hence, Shakespeare's original opening—"My mistress's eyes are nothing like the sun"—becomes "My Mickey Mouse ears are nothing like sonar." Because this is a procedural form, a form on auto-pilot, so to speak—the chance results of which are meant to surprise rather than provoke emotion—this is perhaps the easiest of all constraints to see: the constraint is simply not to compose, given that neither the source material nor the substitutions are the poet's choice.

Mullen's other Shakespearean corruption, "Dim Lady," on the other hand, is a bit trickier to see. This poem also replaces Shakespeare's nouns, yet the constraint is less discernible, because Mullen is simply riffing off of Shakespeare's narrative arc, so that the original—"Coral is far more red than her lips' red"—becomes "Today's special at Red Lobster is redder than her kisser." Though the perceptive reader will easily detect the Shakespearean original in both poems, particularly since the two corruptions appear in the same book, the absurdity of "Variation on a Theme Park" might suggest the imposition of a chance operation—and *Sleeping with the Dictionary* is chockfull of such language games—whereas "Dim Lady" simply uses "My mistress's eyes" as counterpoint, as a historical sparring partner. In consequence, the stricter constraint of "Variation on a Theme Park" is far more discernible.

These poems are not merely whimsical, however, as one unfamiliar with Mullen's book might assume. Indeed, the project itself—to "sleep" with the dictionary (i.e. to *sleep* or *fuck* or *make love to* or *lie dead with* one of the culture's most authoritative texts)—is thrillingly transgressive and politically profound. Like an African American quilt designer who, in Sandra McPherson's words, "reinterpret[s] standard Euro-American motifs . . . [so that] one design may be made to confront another," Mullen trespasses and makes known her presence, as well as the presence of "dark ladies" generally, by writing over or erasing, by word-swapping or -corrupting, canonical and therefore "untouchable" texts (like a Shakespeare sonnet). Mullen's texts declare—behind enemy lines, as it were—: "We're here, too; we, too, have a voice and stake in *this* literature."

But let us return to the principle of discernibility. My "rectangles" seemed to have found a loophole. Set in the typeface (or a closely related typeface) in which they were written, these poems appear as near-perfect rectangles. However, set in any other typeface, the uniform line-length of each poem is entirely lost: the "rectangles" will suddenly resemble typical free verse poems; from a reader's perspective, they will exhibit no discernible constraint at all.

*

For me, the combination of life and reading has provided (so far, at least) almost but not quite enough inspiration. Where inspiration fails, however, constraints can come to the rescue. In the documentary *The Miles Davis Story* (2000), Miles says: "I can't be around a comfortable person. Nothing bounces off them. You get nothing." And I maintain a similar attitude toward my poems—or, more precisely, the act of writing my poems: I need to feel an alert, receptive, tense, even volatile engagement with the material at hand. If inspired or inventive or foreign enough, constraints can steer a writer into startling, unforeseen waters, inciting material even in the face of silence, listlessness, or (most frequent of all, in my experience) confusion.

Where shall I go next? Often this question arises from the sheer number of choices one might make in a poem at any given moment. Dean Young has defined art as "the manifestation of choices in a charged field"—an excellent definition implying that any given piece of art could have been otherwise. So how does a poet of our time, freed from the many traditional constraints of form and rhetoric, choose (or perhaps I should say *settle on*) even a single word from among so many other possible words? In light of this constant dilemma, Flaubert's dictum, *"le mot juste"*—or, "the right word"—seems to me both erroneous and arrogant. Because language is indeed a slippery fish (subjective, mutable, culture-specific, associative, nuanced, hyperbolic, suggestive—this list could go on and on), a poet can only require that his or her choices be, despite all hope for eternal grandeur, merely satisfactory in the moment of composition. This temporary, moment-to-moment satisfaction is precisely what I too require in order to progress from one component of a poem—be it a word or a sentence, a stanza-break or a line-break—to the next.

Thus constraints, even while inciting unexpected results, tend to minimize or simplify our choices, which is just to point out the obvious: constraints exclude, or necessarily include, certain elements of language. The constraint of Bök's *Eunoia* (to exclude certain vowels) limits the possibilities of his diction. Likewise, every word of Matthea Harvey's book-length erasure, *Of Lamb* (2011), has been gleaned from Lord David Cecil's *A Portrait of Charles Lamb* (1983). Or consider Joe Brainard's memoir *I Remember* (1970), an extremist's example of anaphora, in which every sentence begins "I remember . . ." Or Ben Lerner's "Mean Free Path" (2010) in which each stanza, except for its two opening stanzas, contains exactly nine lines. Or Dora Malech's anagrammaniacal *Stet* (2018): "Is it just a word game? / *Is a god just wartime?*" Or Marvin Bell's Dead Man poems, straddling prose and poetry (by making the sentence the poetic line) and challenging our ideas of closure (by offering two texts for each one). Or Magdalena Zurawski's *The Bruise* (2008), a novel that, barring its italicized opening pages, omits commas: 161 pages of comma-less prose. Because so many choices are, in each of these examples, predetermined, the relative constraint tends to facilitate, and therefore often accelerate, the relevant author's forward (avant-) movement.

But I am not suggesting, of course, that limitation guarantees the effectiveness of any given choice. Sometimes a constraint can be too invasive; sometimes a linguistic game of chance (an N+7, say) can produce uninspiring, even boring results. Too, what begins as a formal poem might "end," at least from the reader's perspective, very differently. Constraints may be abandoned midstream, or omitted in revision, or embedded in a larger text (as in "XLII" of David St. John's *The Face*, a free verse poem that contains, within it, a found villanelle, its lines gleaned from Novalis's *Philosophical Writings*). Well, "you can't," as William Stafford said, "be careful and responsible all the time." Things happen—the poem is often a willful child—and the poet adapts. In short, I'm not espousing some authoritative, money-back *ars poetica*. I am merely suggesting that a constraint can be a fruitful challenge, a temporary diversion, and—to the poet as well as to the reader—a source of comfort and delight.

One Take After Another

FRAGMENTS & EPHEMERA

... the act and the potential in the space of the event, in the eventness of the event.
 —Jacques Derrida

I was twelve or thirteen years old when I became—quite without my knowing it—a musician. My age and education being what it was, I would not for many years have access to (or possess the intellectual faculties necessary to access) conventional semantic content: my ideas were musical ideas; my vocabulary was a harmonic vocabulary. In ninth grade, after I performed an original solo bass composition, a woman asked me, "What was that about?" Such a question—about my own or any other non-vocal music—had never occurred to me. It was like being asked, "What was your lunch about?" To say my composition was about an emotion(s) struck me as pompous: I knew even then that artists don't feel more or less deeply than anybody else. And, anyway, the words for emotions ("happiness," "sadness," etc) felt—*still* feel—embarrassingly inadequate. So. I blinked at the woman. "I dunno," I shrugged.

*

The art that matters most to me (and probably to you, too) deepens and enlarges us, teaches us something about the world, and therefore can easily answer the question above.

Easily can I produce thumbnail descriptions of favorite works: *Steve Reich's* Different Trains (1988) *powerfully enacts the experience of traveling in Holocaust trains; Do Ho Suh's* Seoul Home/L.A. Home (1999) *is about homesickness and displacement; Samuel R. Delany's* Time Square Red, Time Square Blue (1999) *is an intelligent and fiercely lived denunciation of gentrification*—and so on and so forth. Nevertheless, the texture and affectivity of living intimately (a phrase plucked from Delany's 1979 memoir *Heavenly Breakfast*) with a given artwork is also part of what it communicates and what it means. I realize now that my twelve- or thirteen-year-old composition was about just this—the sensuous particularity of existing with a few dense minor changes, in a certain region of the fretboard, which is a certain region of the mind, almost imperceptible vibrations spreading from the fingertips outward like rills of warmth . . .

*

I aim to explore in this essay-in-vignettes the phenomenology of my writing—"you think," writes William Matthews, "with your body"—and to bestow prominence to the experiential impact and life appeal of the compositional process, the many series of events in and outside of language that so often lie hidden, for the general reader, in plain sight. An aesthetics caught between act and art. "The poem of the mind in the act of finding / What will suffice" (Wallace Stevens).

*

Last week, over the phone, I asked my father about his erstwhile obsession with rock climbing. (When I was a kid, he climbed nearly every weekend. One of my earliest memories is of him on the toilet, very upright, very focused, practicing knots with a length of neon-green or -yellow rope.) "Sometimes," he told me, his voice dreamy and faintly staticky on the other end of the line, "I felt an insatiable desire to touch rock, to smell sunlight on rock and lichen."

For a few moments the only sound was the squeak of the porchswing on which I slowly swung—phone pressed to my ear.

Which reminded me. In high school, my friends and I loved a skate video called *Listen* (1998) that was soundtrack-less, that featured the raw, unadulterated, unbelievably satisfying sounds of skateboarding. I would sometimes just close my eyes and listen.

*

In college, poet and visual artist truong tran told me that I possessed an erotic relationship to poetry. He conjectured—correctly—that I would like to nuzzle certain words.

*

It is an obvious but much-ignored fact that characters, plots, settings, and speakers are mere illusions, are only as "alive" as their author-creators can convincingly depict them in language. The production and/or consumption of said language, however, constitutes a genuine experience—very much alive (no scare quotes) as it happens. When one of my students asks, as they invariably do, what a particular text is about, I tell them: "For the reader, the text is about the experience of reading the text; for the writer, the text is about the experience of writing it."

*

Or *not* writing it: Years ago, on our way to an open-mic poetry reading, my friend and I found the user manual to a DVD player on the sidewalk. When he was called up to read, he stared straight at me, slowly unfolded the manual, and began to read: *After plugging in the DVD player, press the POWER button . . .*

*

In Tomoka Shibasaki's *Spring Garden* (2014), an illustrator and comic-strip artist named Nishi is obsessed with a "sky-blue house" documented (along with its long-ago residents, a well-known artist couple) in an out-of-print photobook—*Spring Garden*. Taking up residence in a nearby apartment, Nishi stalks the house, later befriending its current residents, in an urgent attempt to behold in person and then to recreate in her art the house's many rooms. As the surrounding Tokyo neighborhood is systematically demolished and rebuilt, Nishi undertakes her updated version of *Spring Garden* and also transmits her obsession to her neighbor, Taro, the novella's protagonist.

Though the book mostly emanates loneliness and loss, I find the iterations of the sky-blue house enlivening. Rather than occupy Shibasaki's characters, the house occupies them, and so survives—a "garden" amidst aggressive urban renewal, a blossoming amidst contemporary urban alienation. Their obsession with the sky-blue house may reveal their lack of satisfactory human engagement, but accumulating versions of it partially eclipse our investment in traditional notions of plot and character, so that readers (or this reader, anyway) partially experience *Spring Garden* as variations on a theme—an unexpectedly warm-blooded exercise/experiment that blurs the divide between art and artifice, between the work (the novella itself) and what philosopher Kendall Walton calls the "work world" (the relevant artwork's imagined world: the dollhouse for the dolls). Variations on the sky-blue house reach beyond the book's fictional domain, creating a palpable interdependency between reader, author, and characters, because they—the variations—are plainly discernible not only as obsessional output arising "naturally" from character and plot, but as compositional input, as one of Shibasaki's central compositional engines, too.

*

In my mid-twenties, when I began to reallocate my artistic energies from music to literature, I found myself drawn to work that reveals or gestures toward its compositional process(es), that makes the texture and affectivity of the writing experience a discernible ingredient of the reading experience. In my own writing, this was and still is an attempt to reignite some of the sensorial mystery and wonder I felt as a kid learning to play electric bass in his bedroom or listening to Coltrane on his father's record player. "I became content to *feel*," writes Baudelaire in "The Exposition Universelle" (1855), "I returned to seek refuge in impeccable *naïveté*."

*

EVENING SKETCHES: AFTER MARVIN BELL

Hands are spreading. Hair is longer. Tongues are
Softer. Legs are glowing. Shadows tangled. Neck
Is longer. Breasts are fuller. Sheets are tangled. Eyes are
Rounder. Arms are slender. Breath is tangled. Body's darker.
Breath is closer. Torso's glowing. Night is fall-
ing. Mouth is open. Sheets are rising. Body's slender.
Hands are fuller. Tongues are spreading. Arms are
Longer. Shadows softer. Eyes are open. Breasts are
Rounder. Neck is slender. Breath is spreading. Body's
Darker. Hair is also. Legs are tangled. Torso's glowing.
Breath is closer. Night is open. Shadows fall-
ing. Hair is spreading. Mouth is open. Hands rising.

Her

voice a sea. Her heart a stone. Her
Song a light. Her throat a bird. Her
Mouth is warm. Her hand a stone. Her
Breath a storm. Her skin is warm. Her
Hair a wave. Her touch a moan. Her

Eyes are spoons. Her breasts arose. Her
Eyes are spoons. Her tongue a bird. Her
Dress a bell. Her waist is air. Her
Skin a dream. Her breasts a moan. Her
Voice a storm. Her song a sea. Her
Touch is stone. Her mouth is light. Her
Hair is air. Her hand a stone. Her
Breath arose. Her breasts as well. Her
Throat is warm. Her tongue is air. Her
Waist a bell. Her heart at sea. Her
Mouth is air. Her voice a dream.

Leather snapping. Louder music. Softer
Whispers. Glowing nightie. Tangled shadows. Louder
Lipstick. Fuller nipples. Tangled breathless.
Rounder faces. Slender torso. Tangled nylon. Haunted
Body. Open fingers. Glowing eyelids. Fall-
ing evening. Whispers rising. Snapping nylon. Slender
Body. Rising leather. Closer breathing. Louder
Torso. Softer shadows. Open faces. Rounder
Nipples. Slender lipstick. Rising breathless. Haunted
Body. Music also. Tangled nightie. Open fingers. Closer
Shadows. Open evening. Fuller music. Fall-
ing breathless. Glowing eyelids. Leather rising.

Our

hands outheld. Your head reclined. Your
Legs aglow. My tongue ignites. Your
Hair unfurls. Your mouth relaxed. My

*Eyes aswim. Your breasts at last. Our
Breath repeats. Your thighs exposed. My
Mind obsessed. Your waist arose. My
Mind obsessed. Your skin ignites. Your
Throat revealed. Our song inside. Your
Breath relaxed. Your dress unfurls. Your
Hair aswim. Your legs are warm. Your
Thighs at last. Your breasts arose. My
Tongue repeats. Your hair aglow. My
Eyes obsessed. My mouth as well. Our
Waists aswim. Your legs outheld. Our
Song revealed. Your head reclined. Your
Thighs are warm. My hands ignite.*

*

I've written a number of poems "after" other poets (Marvin Bell, Ronald Perry, C.D. Wright, Jack Gilbert, Johann Wolfgang von Goethe) that strike me as especially (poly)sensuous. Not only do they evoke for me the gazillion hours I have spent on the floor of a dimly lighted room, practicing scales, patterns, exercises, and études; not only is my love for these poets discernible as ghosted materiality, as language haunting formal systems—they also very nearly abandon meaning for sound. I think often, in fact, of a dream (an *actual* dream: I keep a notebook beside my bed) in which my laptop keyboard was a piano keyboard, and words were chords, and each letter could be sharped or flatted at will.

I am reminded again and again that what distinguishes my current poetic practice from the musical practice of my youth is that, today, I no longer regard practice as a means to an end (i.e. a way of perfecting or maintaining skills) but rather as an end in itself. The abovementioned poems in particular are not unlike improvisational exercises recorded late at night, over a demitasse of espresso or a snifter of cognac, one take after another, imperfections and all . . .

*

Mark Strand: "It is the oddity of our poems, their idiosyncrasy, their lapses into a necessary awkwardness, their ultimate frailty, that charms and satisfies."

*

In Chapter 17 of Mark Twain's *Huckleberry Finn* (1885), Huck examines an unfinished crayon drawing by recently deceased Emmeline Grangerford. It features "a young woman in a long white gown, standing on the rail of a bridge all ready to jump . . . looking up at the moon, with tears running down her face." However, because Emmeline died before she could finish "her greatest picture," this young woman has "two arms folded across her breast, and two arms stretched out in front, and two more reaching up towards the moon": Emmeline planned "to see which pair would look best and then scratch out all the other arms." Though Twain was clearly satirizing the comic seriousness of popular 19th-century tragic romances, E.W. Kemble and John Harley's original illustration (see below) of this young woman is neither tragic nor comic. Instead, it's metamorphic: a woman with six semi-transparent arms—"so many arms it made her look too spidery." Emmeline's failure to settle on one pair of arms inadvertently produced a new and decidedly unromantic heroine. She is a spider woman *and* a plural subject reaching simultaneously in different directions.

"IT MADE HER LOOK SPIDERY."

*

Maya Catherine Popa: "I learned to listen to variations."

*

"Art is the manifestation of choices in a charged field," contends Dean Young in *The Art of Recklessness*, and I relish writing that pluralizes those choices, that "fails" to construct the illusion of a literary world in which only one pair of arms ever existed or could exist. "[I]n our time, to perceive, comprehend, or apprehend any object, the preceptor must accumulate a variety of perspectives upon that object. He must 'see' it" — I'm quoting from Sharon Spencer's *Space, Time, and Structure in the Modern Novel* (1971) — "from as many points of view as possible." When Marvin Bell told me that he'd once borrowed Donald Justice's office and there, in a desk drawer, found numerous sheets of paper on which a couplet had been obsessively written and rewritten and then rewritten again, I knew I was supposed to be impressed by the older poet's patience, care, precision: the time-honored "struggle" for perfection. Instead, I found the (imagined) record of the couplet's composition — its accumulation of perspectives — far more captivating than any single "final" couplet could be. "The house of fiction has . . . not one window, but millions" (Henry James).

*

Wong Kar-wai's *In the Mood of Love* (2000): a film about a man named Chow (Tony Leung Chiu-wai) and a woman named Su (Maggie Cheung Man-yuk) who discover their respective partners are having an affair and are thus propelled into each other's arms. Fascinatingly, the film features a number of back-to-back scenes repeated with a difference: Night. A deserted Hong Kong street. Their shadows stretched across a concrete wall. Chow takes Su's hand, says, "Perhaps we shall stay out tonight?" and Su turns away. Then: Night. A deserted Hong Kong street. Their shadows stretched across a concrete wall. Su smiles coquettishly, grazes her fingers against the bottom edge of Chow's sportscoat, and then turns away as before. We don't know which of the two scenes actually happened, if either of them did. "After all," says Chow, as though commenting on the film itself, "it has already happened. It doesn't matter who made the first move."

*

Then again, I do sometimes want a narrative to do something other than what it does, seeing as most narratives do not offer multiple takes . . .

Yesterday, on my porch, I read the passage in Ellen Douglas's 1973 Southern Gothic novel *Apostles of Light* in which Dr. Lucas Alexander, out for a stroll, looks up to see the senile Mrs. Crane on the balcony above him with "an expression of serious resolution on her face, her cane raised above her head in both hands and swung back above her shoulder very much as a baseball player holds a bat." Wanting the novel to double down on its gothic horror, on its haunted house-cum-nursing home setting, I was a little disappointed when Mrs. Crane merely struck herself three times on the head and crumpled to the brick floor, concussed. I wanted her to throw herself over the balcony, ritual suicide-style, like the old married couple in Ari Aster's *Midsommar* (2019).

A few days later, reading the novel's final chapter, the ghost of my imagined scene returned. Flat on her hospital bed, Mrs. Crane tells Lucas that she had wanted to die, still does, but is now too weak even to execute it. "'There's not even a window high enough to jump out of,'" she says.

*

EVENING SKETCH: AFTER JACK GILBERT

music of sagebrush   cold night of night-   mares
     curtains of winter-   long   stories of hair
of breathing   pianos / black   teeth of nightmares
     flash o' lightning   of swimming, & bodies
of air   voices of backroads   our shadows of breathing
    smoke of twin harps / our   shadows of swimming
     a bowl of white hair   the monk escapes of-
ten   sweat of more sweat: the music   of breathing
sagebrush of backroads   the twin   harps of swimming
     the black teeth of smoke / cold   winter of
    lightning   air of pianos   long night of night-
     mares   phosphor of oranges   pianos
her hair   black / curtains of voices   a white bowl
     of cold   flash   stories of bodies
of breathing back-   roads   sweat of more sweat,
     the monk hides despair   flash o' nightmares
of bodies   of black teeth   & stories   twin
shadows of light- / ning-   long   music of hair

*

Recently, writing poems "after" Jack Gilbert, I employ an admittedly unusual procedure: I pluck words from his *Collected Poems* and insert them quite at random into a form I developed, a form built upon the repetition of words/ phrases separated by a single preposition (e.g. "breathless *through* windstorms"; "blood *through* ripped sheets"; "drift-leaves *through* keyholes"; etc). The product of this procedure becomes the raw material out of which the sketch is made.

Gilbert, I suspect, would roll his eyes at such a process. And yet it's a process whereby I consistently access—even if the sketches are not consistently successful—that which I love most about his own poetry: his embrace of both the insufficiency of language ("How astonishing it is that language can almost mean, / and frightening that it does not quite") and the inescapable fact that language fairly hums—*always* hums?—with resonant meanings ("What we feel most has / no name but amber, archers, cinnamon, horses and birds").

*

An editor once remarked upon my own repetition of words: *dark, body, hair, shadow, night.* I had to admit I *do* love these words, even if—or maybe precisely *because*—it makes me feel like a brooding teenager plunking minor chords on a piano, sustain pedal to the metal.

*

William Carlos Williams: "a poem is a small (or large) machine made out of words."

*

When writing an ongoing series, "Lineage: 7 Variations," John Coltrane is often on my mind (and stereo). Specifically, I think of his talent for extending phrases beyond their expected conclusions, for broadening and/or artfully complicating the improvisational units of which his solos were composed. In one well-known anecdote, Coltrane, defending the length of his solos, tells Miles, "I can't find a way to stop," to which Miles replies, "You might start by taking the horn out of your fucking mouth." Channeling the spirit of Coltrane, each "Lineage" variation is a single-paragraph story (with one exception—I cannot refuse the opportunity to break "rules") comprised of extended, hypotactic sentences, which I rather fancifully regard as "sheets of sound," the now-famous term Ira Gitler used to describe Coltrane's solos. Each "Lineage" variation is loath to place periods or close paragraphs, is loath to take the horn out of its fucking mouth.

*

Some fifteen years ago, I recorded a duet with my longtime childhood bass instructor, Mike Kelly, entitled "Audio Wallpaper." It featured a technique known as "tapping" in which both hands engage the fretboard—imagine each of us playing his bass as though it were a piano—and repeated subtle melodic variations ad infinitum. In truth, the composition reflected our predominant practice method: we would repeat a riff in unison until we entered a trance-like state in which we (I'll speak for both of us here) felt the mental "stress" of the activity slowly dissolve and our minds awaken inside the music—"the strange world of sounds," wrote Borges "—the strangest world of art"—two figures floating perfectly still inside a storm cloud. In this way, too, the sheet-of-sound/audio-wallpaper impulse (not to mention the degree-of-difficulty calculation that contributes to my pursuit of it) is quite deeply engrained in me.

*

Can readers discern in this prose text the spirit of Coltrane specifically? I doubt it—and I don't care. Art is chockfull of present absences. Yet readers can indeed discern that the sentential maneuvering of "Lineage: 7 Variations" is rooted in the practice of jazz improvisation. The basic sentence structures of each variation are almost identical; together, they form the chord progression over which I can solo, the skeleton over which I can drape sundry clothes.

*

RITORNELLO (OR, LANDSCAPE WITH X)

In the newest version,
      you're stumbling through shrubland,
 Having never listened (from your seaside window) to either her violin
Or her running bathwater.
       There's only a mindless longing
 For the edge, or the sound beyond the edge, like the soughing of wind
Through her eyelashes.
      Hours of parched-throat stumbling,
Then hours of euphoric meditation.
        Just ignore the unsettling moment
 When, stumbling along beside yourself, watching yourself,
Your hands (like her scarlet negligees) become transparent,
          indicating
 That the transformation has begun: you're almost prepared
To live in the dirt, ascetic, thinning the rust-colored shrubs.
         Charming,

I think, even if her Puccini albums, from an earlier version,
Haunt your dreams. Soon you'll be listening

                                      to green stems squealing
Out of the sun-bleached earth, and what more do you need?
Life is cranberries and a busted watch. Happiness,

                                        like a hatful of rain,
Gushes over you. You can't even hear her washing lettuce
In a metal sink, singing an aria from

                             (let me guess) *Tosca? La bohème?*

*

Once, over coffee, M. asked me why didn't I write more poems about jazz? Though jazz and jazz musicians receive occasional spotlight, my poetry is unequivocally dominated by classical music. Gazing down into my half-empty mug of coffee, I proceeded to tell M. that I loved classical music and that I grew up on the Russians: Rachmaninoff, Stravinsky, Shostakovich. Which is just to say I didn't answer her question. I didn't tell her that Miles listened almost exclusively to classical music, as his records with Bill *and* Gil Evans attest—"He played Khachaturian, Debussy, Chopin," says Frances Taylor Davis, Miles' first wife, in the 2001 documentary *The Miles Davis Story*—or that my go-to process of composition is essentially bop-derived:

Owing to my background as a workaday jazz musician (I played out of a fakebook in the DeWald-Taylor Quintet for over a decade), it feels perfectly ordinary for me to open a "finished" text and improvise, so to speak, over its changes. Our charge as musicians was to—in accordance with Pound—"make new" tunes we'd played, let alone heard in recordings, ten thousand times. "[I]nstant variety and instant repetition," wrote Italo Calvino in his introduction to *Italian Folktales*. Every instantiation of a tune must be a new tune and the same old tune, both.

*

ROUND MIDNIGHT

Frances and I were perched on the windowsill, passing a stogie back and forth, watching the rain pour slantwise in the neon-purple night. Prokofiev's *Symphony No. 1* spun on the turntable. Images of *The Outer Limits* flickered like an eerie slideshow upon the walls. I rested my hand on her thigh. It felt like touching somebody else's sentimental photograph. She just picked up my hand and placed it in my lap again. "You're in the wrong key, honey," she whispered.

"I'm a key dangling from a thundercloud."

She uncrossed her legs as if to stand but she did not. Miles' horn issued from the kitchen—a few Egyptian-sounding notes, middle range and legato. Cigar smoke hovered in the air like a charmed cobra. My partner, I knew, lay wide awake in our dark bedroom. And now for the moment when she will lift the damp blue cloth from her face . . .

*

In his final book, *Palm-of-the-Hand Stories* (1988), Yasunari Kawabata famously rewrites his most celebrated novel, *Snow Country* (1948), as a five-page short story.

*

Several months ago, I decided to show my son and daughter a made-for-TV movie I'd watched again and again as a young child—*Ewoks: The Battle of Endor* (1985). I hadn't seen it in over thirty years, and watching it now between my kids on our overstuffed gray sofa, I realized that I remembered nothing about plot, character, or dialogue; yet the sound of pie tins and of actors eating with wooden spoons and bowls was intensely evocative, issuing as it was from the past and the present at the same time.

*

If a traditional lyric poem ("the spontaneous overflow of powerful emotions recollected in tranquility," as Wordsworth so famously put it) is a memorial to a single human's experience of a discrete moment on earth, then I'm interested in a hall-of-mirrors lyric, in a lyric for collectivists, in the lyric as a site in which one can repeatedly access, tranquilly or no, discrete moments on earth, understanding full well that one has been here (or somewhere all too like it) at least once before.

*

Vladimir Propp: "The names of the dramatic personae change (as well as the attributes of each), but neither their actions nor functions change. From this we can draw the inference that a tale often attributes identical actions to various personages."

*

Or perhaps the *same* personage, à la Chris Marker's *La Jetée* (1962). A 28-minute *photo-roman* composed almost entirely of black-and-white film stills and narrated with spare, trickily precise voiceover, *La Jetée* concerns a nameless man (Davos Hanich) who travels back in time in search of the moment in which he, as a child, witnessed the death of a man on the pier of Orly Airport, Paris. Yet he realizes only years later that he had witnessed a man dying; what he remembers—the image that has "marked" him and thus made him a candidate for time travel—is a woman's face at the end of the pier, a seemingly ordinary, if beautiful, face that would remain with him throughout World War Three and beyond, "a unique image of peacetime." At film's end, having traveled back in time to his childhood afternoon at Orly Airport, he runs toward the woman at the end of the pier, but is suddenly shot and killed by a man from the future secretly trailing him: Our protagonist had, as a child, witnessed his own death.

Which reminds me. Also in 1962, Italian writer Natalia Ginzburg published a book of essays called *Le Piccole Virtù* (*The Little Virtues*). In her essay "He and I," she relates how her husband, the scholar and screenwriter Gabriele Baldini, drove them for hours through foggy identical suburbs in search of a cinema "showing a film from the 1930s, about the French Revolution, which he had seen as a child, and in which a famous actress of that time appeared for a moment or two." Fifteen minutes into the film, however, the actress had come and gone, and already Baldini wanted to leave, despite his wife's wish to finish the film—they'd driven all this way to watch it, after all. On the drive home, when Ginzburg asked him how the film would end, he told her that "the story wasn't at all important, the only thing that mattered was those few moments, that actress's curls, gestures, profile."

*

When I first read Propp's *Morphology of the Folktale* (1928)—a study in which Russian fairy tales are broken into and analyzed as thematic and narratological chunks, which tend to be, Propp discovers, sequenced in particular ways—I thought of the gazillion hand-me-down phrases/patterns that jazz musicians lean on (mostly for practical reasons, as when a player needs a brief mental or physical break from intensity, a gulp of air before diving back down into the depths) during solos. I glimpsed in Propp's *Morphology* a way to produce narratives that excused stock phrases/patterns as part and parcel of a general practice. Rather than attribute "identical actions to various personages," however, "Lineage: 7 Variations" attributes various actions in identical or almost identical sentence structures: "My grandmother's alone, more alone than I, though less alone than my grandfather . . ."; "I'm handsome—a bit handsomer, I think, than my brother—but perhaps not quite as handsome as our father . . ."; "My father's a very fine musician—a better musician, at least, than my uncle, who will strum his guitar and croon to old wide-hipped ladies in the subway, like a troubadour—though he's not nearly as fine a musician as my wife . . ." And so on and so forth.

*

Vikram Seth: "[T]he variations take on a strange, mysterious distance, as being, in a sense, variations one degree removed, orchestral variations on variations."

*

Repeated, the technical elements acquire an uncanniness: one senses the present absence of an urtext—"something," to quote Freud, "which is secretly familiar." And indeed there *is* an urtext. In 2012, I published a very short story called "Lineage" that contained the "original" sentential skeleton of the series. Though the story itself was forgettable, the movement of its sentences gnawed at me, haunted me, as though the form was always already uncanny. *Here,* I intuited, *is a template for producing plot and conflict*—two essential narrative elements for which I have little to no natural ability or interest. Still, for reasons unclear to me, a number of years would pass before I, bored and alone in a fluorescent-lighted college computer lab ("boredom," claims Carmine Starnino "is the highest state of creativity"), wrote the first "Lineage" variation.

*

I disclose the mechanics of "Lineage: 7 Variations" in the text(s) itself so that readers will reflect on the act of writing even as they engage with character and plot; that they will regard the disclosure as indiscreet and in conflict with the supremacy of autonomous finished texts; and that they will seek narrative connections (*Are these characters members of a single family, each variation a branch of one big family's tree?*)

as well as morphological connections (*Do particular words, phrases, and sentence structures appear and reappear like strands of linguistic DNA across the series? Are these variations quite literally blood-related?*)

*

2.19.72

pool of blood-red blood we see ourselves knelt round Lee Morgan his shivering wife in whom we see ourselves the gun outthrust his wife so tiny in his fur coat the gun outthrust red-handed on the floor of Slugs' red- handed we are silence in the New York streets on the floor of Slugs' silence in the neon green snow- fall when his wife shot him I hummed "You Go to My Head" snow- fall flying high we were far-off sirens flying high we were an ambulance caught in the snow in the snow our heads spinning *Search for the New Land* in the bell of his trumpet our heads spinning his wife's reflection caught her in his fur coat in the bell of his trumpet her melted face still listening to you play her melted face knelt round Lee Morgan still listening to you play pool of blood-red blood

*

In *Ask Your Mama: 12 Moods of Jazz* (1961), Langston Hughes includes an afterword, "Liner Notes," which consists of an "informative" prose paragraph for each poem in the collection. Addressed to *"the poetically unhep,"* these paragraphs read like prose poems, so rich are they in Hughes' rhymes and rhythms: "Because grandma lost her apron with all the answers in her pocket (perhaps consumed by fire) certain grand- and- great-grandsons play music burning like dry ice against the ear. Forcing cries of succor from its own unheard completion—not resolved by Charlie Parker—can we look to monk or Monk? Or let it rest with Eric Dolphy?" Instead of over-explaining or speaking down to *"the poetically unhep"* —a white audience ignorant of his many black cultural references—Hughes refuses to "speak" inauthentically. Because the tinge of anger and frustration is arguably more apparent in the afterword than in the lineated poems, "Liner Notes" extends the book's genre *and* emotion, a series of corresponding prose poems in a darker mood: a shadow of the book as a whole. In Hughes I rediscovered that structure and form can facilitate, in the rep-and-rev tradition, not only a more expansive range of emotional and tonal registers, but a more intricate blurring of poetry and prose.

*

There is an opening from one room to the next . . .

Barbara Tomash's "Home Stead," from *The Secret of White* (2009), contains a final, coda-like stanza. Separated from the poem proper by an asterisk, this "coda" is also tonally distinct: observational, existential, and slightly formal in its use of the first-person plural: *we walk between the two without thinking, we cross the boundary between living and dying . . .*

"Like commentary on the poem itself," I told her one afternoon in her office.

Barbara looked at me and nodded. She said many rabbis believe a text does not exist unless it's been commented on.

*

Tuscan proverb: "The tale is not beautiful if nothing is added to it."

*

Composing from scratch—*creatio ex nihilo*—is neither the greater method nor the greater skill; it's instead a different method and skill, one in which each decision is guided by (1) a large-scale conception of the urtext, (2) an intuitive inkling of what the in-progress text will be, and (3) the real-time communion of risk and grace (i.e. the ability to gracefully maneuver formal attributes as well as surprise, break expectations, reach "beyond your formulas" [Charles Mingus]). Though my writing is not, strictly speaking, improvised— language doesn't pour spontaneously out of me, à la David Antin's "talk poems"—my baseline compositional process foregrounds skills and tenets particularly revered by the jazz improviser. I often pursue highly formal/structured poems (and prose texts) solely for the fun of "playing" against their rules.

*

"[T]he unexpected within the parameters of the anticipated," said Julio Cortázar.

*

LINES

awake to snowfall in the over-   lighted room your father's trumpet angling upward   wailing red-cheeked in your childhood mirror a sound   like brass birds burst in your red mirror shattered as from a tree upward   into the snow suspended as from a burst you hear rumbling up under your fingers rumbling up in-   side a bassline which like a ghost train reaches inside touches your father   a ghost through a phonograph over-   touches your father   closed-eyed lowering his horn   listens then in his gauze-white shirt then begins   to play again a lifelong echo begins his sound unfolding a life   under your bassline a star chart begin unfolding shattered you hear over-   head like a star walking at dusk you cannot not hear your father's trumpet   amidst the silent mountains   awake to snow-   fall

*

Because language occurs, unlike music, non-simultaneously—"The story is what happens in the reader's mind as his eyes move from the first word to the second, the second to the third, and so on to the end of the tale," writes Delany in his essay "About 5,750 Words"—the kind of risk-taking mentioned above is only discernible via juxtaposition: the juxtaposition between the poems in Hughes' *Ask Your Mama* and their corresponding liner notes, for example. To discern the riskiness, to register the extent to which this or that decision challenges/strays from the predictable, the reader has to approximate simultaneity by reading the urtext (or any previous instantiation of a text) *behind* or *alongside* its variant. Each compositional decision bears a history. Thus, alternative versions of the text are discernible palimpsestically—a palpable present absence, or extra-textual energy, affecting our reading experience. *The texture and affectivity of living intimately with a given artwork.*

*

Cassie Donish: "The memory is a beautiful ghost"

*

inside him for years a river of her brown hair floating round organs as he walks silent a river of her brown hair under sulfur lamps as he walks silent his shadow reaches backward under sulfur lamps clutching a moment his shadow reaches backward *we woke before dawn* clutching a moment *you uncased your violin* before dawn they woke scarfed & pea-coated she uncased her violin threaded a long note through air scarfed & pea-coated so that they remain threaded a long note through air in the yellow room so that they remain huddled a present absence in the yellow room twin ghost-plumes of breath huddled a present absence even as he walks twin ghost-plumes of breath to their candlelit table even as he walks feeling the four walls to their candlelit table he hums to himself feeling the four walls the sound of her in his mouth he hums to himself she's right here again *the sound of you in my mouth* against her shoulder she's right here again her bow pulling the note taut against her shoulder he presses his lips her bow pulling the note taut & his eyes squeeze shut he presses his lips in cheap wine her reflection & his eyes squeeze shut floating round organs in cheap wine her reflection tumbling cold transparent for years inside him

*

At the center of truong tran's *four letter words* (2008) are four barely visible poems—ghost poems—printed on both sides of two sheets of transparent vellum. *Are these dead poems? Poems "abandoned," as Valéry might put it, too early? Were they once (or once intended to be) something else?* And perhaps most importantly: *What are they now, together, layered almost illegibly one upon the other?*

*

I first encountered the cinematographic photography of Jeff Wall at his SFMOMA retrospective exhibition in 2007. Even more than his imaginative ideas (*The Flooded Grave*, 1998-2000) or technical prowess (*A Sudden Gust of Wind* [After Hokusai], 1993), the uncanniness of his pictures utterly overwhelmed me. Approximately life-sized but mounted in brighter-than-life lightboxes, Wall's photographs are almost exclusively set-constructed. Chancing upon an event or location of pictorial interest, he does not photograph it, but rather stages it and hires actors to inhabit the space. Hence, his well-known mantra: "I begin by *not* photographing." Which is just to say that Wall doesn't march lockstep within a documentary-based tradition of photography, shooting the world as it exists. Instead, he behaves as a documentary photographer of collaborative semi-controlled environments, merely observing, merely waiting to "capture"—well, *something*.

In photography as in poetry: "What the poem is," as John Ciardi writes in *How Does a Poem Mean?* (1959), "is inseparable from its own performance of itself."

*

With the exception of several centerpieces (a koi pond, a brick patio, a few well-placed canopy trees), my father's backyard has been continually reimagined. At present, it's a veritable rainforest featuring two ponds, three waterfalls, a stream, three patios, one sunken patio, cushioned benches, hanging lanterns, windchimes, a labyrinth of stone paths, a quivering overlay of shadow—in short, not what one expects of a modestly-sized, tract home backyard in the middle of suburbia. And yet, despite its many relaxing, transportive properties, I'm most intrigued by the yard's history and perpetual as-yet-unfinishedness, the way in which family and friends cannot *not* experience the yard as process rather than as product. Because earlier versions of the yard are visible palimpsestically—I can still see the gazeboed hot tub over here, the chain-linked dog den over there, and over there the wooden footbridge—the (re)experience is one of fullness and of absence, both. Variability contributes as much to my father's backyard as water, light, or air.

*

To reimagine a text is to challenge traditional notions of *closure, totalization, finality, perfection*—aesthetic tenets in which I put zero stock. If I *did* believe in them, then perhaps I would relinquish art altogether and be satisfied replacing batteries in my children's toys. As Marvin Bell likes to tell his students (I was one of them—one of ten thousand to have crept out from under his overcoat): "It's not work, and it's never finished." I want to create art that engenders a sense of never-endingness.

*

I'm currently writing another ongoing series, "To an Imagined Us," the component parts of which are neither numbered (suggesting linearity) nor titled (suggesting independence), but rather separated by glyphs (suggesting assemblage—a series of parts, or [re]movable pieces, quite various in my case, gathered under a single banner). My hope is that "To an Imagined Us" will be read kaleidoscopically—the second part echoes the fifth part, the eighth part echoes the fourteenth part, the sixth part echoes the eighteenth part, and so on— with the understanding that neither the order nor the quantity of parts/pieces matters. "There's no truth," writes Deborah A. Miranda in her poem-story "Formula," "in the old formula of beginning, middle, end." My hope is that its component sections are interchangeable, are what Sharon Spencer would call a "mobile construct"—its structure "constitutes a denial of linear chronology" and is "dependent upon juxtaposition [as] the chief means by which the impression of 'mobility' is attained."

*

Joshua Jennifer Espinoza: "Nothing is unrelated."

*

In March, Mike Kelly, my bass instructor, died of pancreatic cancer at the age of fifty-seven. After I heard the news, I lay on the floor of our darkened bedroom with my bass flat across my chest—not performing for him, but practicing. (It turns out grief, too, is a sheet of sound.) Trying to make him proud. As though I would arrive, once more, at his house after school on Tuesday.

*

NOCTURNE (OR, LANDSCAPE WITH FATHER)

We can no longer stand in the clearing, in the naked woods,
Letting the Oregon mist seep through our clothes—
Our father, under his green afghan, is summoning Hubbard,
Blue Spirits, as though to make us face ourselves
(Swollen-eyed, ill-shaven) in the plastic slips of his records.
Ashbery said: "We live in the sigh of our present"—

But we can no longer even believe in time: we are kneeling
In our bedroom, thumbing through album covers;
At the same moment, we are slogging through delphiniums
To see our father, silhouetted, practicing Hsing I
On a wooden bridge. Ah, here it is: *Blue Spirits*. Our father
Lifting one liver-spotted hand, as the needle falls
Into the groove, as the wide leaves flush too soon, too soon . . .
Can we turn back, later, after he has died, to live
With silence and black coffee, to amble over the stone path
In our sockfeet, our threadbare robe, considering
Our next unpredictable gesture, like hacking up firewood
On a floor of mirrors? The question is ridiculous—
We can no longer leave this house, this music: we will live
Beside him, on this folding chair, reading Auden.
Even in Poros, years later, grating lemon over grilled squid,
We will prop him up to watch reruns of *Bonanza*.
Meanwhile, we are listening to Hubbard, whose music fills
This house and this house alone, though we hear,
Under a sun-reddened parasol, for example, faint overtones
That make us close our eyes. Our father is dying—
Nothing stopping it. Yet here he is, for the moment, patting
The green afghan, his once-heroic legs, standing
Moreover in an abandoned farmhouse: the sound of a horn
Lost among the rooms, the nothingness of rooms,
And we can no longer find it for him, our father: he is gone—

*

When I was an undergraduate at San Francisco State University, Camille Dungy took a prose poem of mine and reordered all of its sentences—an experiment that taught me so much about part-whole relations and the importance of angular "turns." It was like listening to Thelonious Monk play stride for the first time: the experiment revealed to me that Dungy dug my poems (very heartening indeed), but also poked fun at a certain quaintness or tidiness they possessed.

I thought of this event the other afternoon, at the playground sandbox, when my son sang the Alphabet Song at the top of his lungs—"A, B, C, D, F, I, G . . ."—and two older girls stared up at their mom, wide-eyed, then pointed at my son and shouted: "That's wrong! That's wrong! He's singing it wrong!" Wrong? Protectively, I wanted to inform them that the order of the letters scarcely matters. More importantly, anyway, he sang the song correctly—in rhythm and right on key.

*

A great many of my poems are what my friend d. calls "rectangles"—that is, poems with lines of uniform length, thus resembling near-perfect rectangles. These are written on a word processor, in Times New Roman, with a margin ruler (no justified margins). Each poem was unique, but appeared uncannily similar to the others. At a glance, they seemed to emerge as from a factory, a succession of rectangular text-objects. Variations on a visual theme. *Maybe,* I thought, *I would print them on cardstock, cut them out, and collect them as I used to collect baseball cards as a kid.*

*

Working so meticulously with the margin ruler, I made-believe these rectangles had one foot in a minimalist tradition. Geometric "studies" such as Josef Albers' *Homage to the Square* series (1950-1976) induced me, in fact, to write poems with different sets of lines of uniform length and/or with unconventional layouts. But more important than line-length uniformity is my love for the tactility of measuring, the treatment of language as physical material, and texts that are as much (set-)constructed as they are composed.

*

2 LANDSCAPES: AN OPERA

Only in opera do angels need skin.
    —Richard Powers

1. *Her*
Sour coffee, the plush seats of the dining car, the night snow
    Over the Nebraska fields, and still she remembers him
Praising her legs, the slender calves, among the white stones
    Of the shore. Staring at her reflection in the dark glass,
Hoping he is not watching her. Sipping the last of her coffee,
    Then almost spitting up with laughter when her mouth
Fills with grinds. She longs to be alone, on this droning train,
    With her earthly pleasures: snow piling on farmhouses,
On the backs of cows, humming the Queen of the Night aria,
    The tablecloth strewn with packets of cream and sugar.

And then, in her mind, in the copper-green light, his feathers
> Brushing her naked breasts. Can she unremember him,
The baritone voice, the pointed tongue, in order to feel alone,
> On earth, with a cup of coffee? She smiles in the glass,
Admiring the grinds in her teeth and gums, which, of course,
> He would never understand. Dead-of-winter cornfields
And *Don Giovanni* in her head. Perhaps he ought to see this—
> *For what, more than inadequacies, will turn him away?*

2. Him

> Come on, slugger,

No more dragging your wings over the pearlescent beach—
You are not made for sulking. You can smell the banquet,
> The supple meats,

And you choose to be with rocks and phosphorous waves . . .
Where's your gusto, your triumphant good cheer? Voices
> Urging you home

From the green mountains, singing *Paradise and the Peri*,
While you disappear into the mind, into the lush begonias,
> Her humid thighs

Around your waist. She has lived, all winter, without you—
Eating cold noodles with peanut sauce—and still you fail
> To heave the past

Into the sea. What kind of angel wanders the beach alone,
Reliving bedroom scenes? You grip your toes in the sand,
> Remember Casals

Lighting on Bach's Cello Suites in a Barcelona thrift store,
Then breathing them to life, after two centuries of silence . . .
> That's outrageous—

To compare your past to a piece of music, while the choir

>   Of the green mountains, singing for you, under the palms,
>   In the fading light,
>   Goes unlistened-to. Perhaps you can examine her forever—
>   *A white torso in the purple grass*—but sometime, slugger,
>   The song will end.

*

Allen Ginsberg frequently and experimentally altered the size of his notebooks. The size would often determine the length of his poetic lines. Because improvisation often grows out of such random gambits, it feels quite natural for me to follow an arbitrary line-length, whether it be predetermined (à la Ginsberg's notebooks), established by an opening line, or both.

*

If I were to spread a smattering of my poems here before you, dear reader, would you be able to identify which are the rectangles and which are not?

*

When I received the galleys for my first published rectangle, I frowned, I sulked. It was not a near-perfect rectangle. Improvidently, I hadn't realized that the uniform line-length of these poems, when set in almost any font other than Times New Roman, would be entirely lost. Now, however, I love that my poems possess a "secret" methodology. I look forward to the moment when I, as opposed to an editor, set a new poem in a different font, suddenly creating the jagged right margin, the instantaneous erosion of its vertical rockface. I feel like my son, who builds humungous multicolored block towers ("Sooooo tall," he exclaims, standing on tiptoe, stretching up his arms) solely for the fun of knocking them down.

*

Bookending truong tran's *four letter words* are "paragraphs" of some dingbat font (numbers, images, unintelligible glyphs) with short phrases appearing, erasure-style, throughout. Asked about it, truong said these pages were not-so-successful poems that nevertheless contributed greatly to his understanding of the book. Rather than excise them, he performed an erasure on them and disguised them as idiosyncratic (and mostly visual) front and back matter.

*

If one denies, as I do, totalization and closure, if one "resist[s] a notion of art as capable of seeing beyond," as Halberstam writes in *The Queer Art of Failure*, then one ought to reframe one's relationship to one's art—one ought to empower art's confined space (a backyard, a "rectangle," a reconstruction of an event *not* photographed) by equating movement within it as emancipatory. Like a jazz musician, one ought to treat the limitations or boundaries of one's art less as confinement than as an opportunity to challenge, transform, expand, resist, reinvent.

*

For me, this "confinement" is also a mindfulness technique whereby the lack of physical space has forced (or tricked) me into an embodied awareness of the present moment. As one might expect, the sensuousness of writing becomes dramatically heightened.

*

A few semesters ago, in a literature-based composition course, my students and I discussed the queer, uncanny space of Jim and Harriet Stone's apartment in Raymond Carver's "Neighbors" (1970). More *Twilight Zone* than Dirty Realism, "Neighbors" is the story of Bill and Arlene Miller, "a happy couple" who agree to "look after the Stones' apartment, feed Kitty, and water the plants," only to discover, separately, that the apartment changes them: they re-costume themselves ("He stepped into the panties and fastened the brassier"); become distracted, removed from ordinary time ("'I didn't feed Kitty or do any watering.' She looked at him. 'Isn't that stupid?'"); and carry the trace-marks—the psychosexual aftereffects—of it back to their own apartment/lives:

> She let him use her key to open the door. He looked at the door across the hall before following her inside.
> "Let's go to bed," he said.
> "Now?" She laughed. "What's gotten into you?"
> "Nothing. Take your dress off." He grabbed for her awkwardly, and she said, "Good God, Bill."
> He unfastened his belt.

I regard the story as a metaphor for the excitement and artistic possibility (and felt potentiality) of entering extant narratives. In the uncanny alternate reality of the Stones' apartment, Bill and Arlene's allegiance to their own narrative promptly malfunctions, and Carver commences a close study—a Jeff Wall-like observation—of characters over whom he holds, or pretends he holds, no dominion: "[Bill] moved slowly through each room considering everything that fell under his gaze, carefully, one object at a time." Rather than escape his aesthetic proclivities by looking *out*, Carver queers the fictive space of the Stones' apartment: he "resist[s] a notion of art as capable of seeing beyond." Though the Millers, at story's end, accidentally lock themselves out of the Stones' apartment, Carver has nevertheless made contact with his (non-realist) literary "neighbors," has already freed himself, however briefly, from the limitations of realism's prevailing aesthetic conventions.

*

In high school, my friends and I skateboarded from the instant the last bell rang until it grew dark outside, moving from one "spot" to another only when we bored of it or when (more commonly) we got kicked out. Twenty years later I still maintain a skater's view of the world: stairs, rails, ledges, gaps, well-lit empty lots—indeed the entire urban landscape—is a skate park, a series of spots. For street skaters, concrete jungles are charged not only with possibility (what has been or can be done) but with potentiality (what can be imagined or may be done in the future).

*

My rock-climbing father would understand. Once, in midtown Sacramento—I must have been seven or eight years old—I watched, enthralled, as he began to scale the rock façade of what was, if memory serves, a frozen yogurt shop.

Which reminds me. Once, for a week or so, my high school skater friends and I played a video game, a race car game, in which we never raced, but instead played SKATE (the skateboard equivalent of basketball's HORSE) by variously flipping our cars on steep hills well outside of the prescribed racetrack. "If you can't dream up worlds that might be, then you are limited to the worlds other people describe," write Robert and Michèle Root-Bernstein.

*

Or, as José Esteban Muñoz puts it in *Cruising Utopia: The Then and There of Queer Futurity* (2009): "Possibilities exist, or more nearly, they exist within a logical real, the possible, which is within the present and is linked to presence. Potentialities are different in that although they are present, they do not exist in present things. Thus, potentialities have a temporality that is not in the present but, more nearly, in the horizon, which we can understand as futurity. Potentiality is and is not presence . . ."

*

I view a page of text, too, as a series of spots—a site in which to attempt possibilities and to evoke, in readers' and writers' minds alike, potentialities: "the warm illumination of a horizon" (Muñoz), the ghostly presence of what is not written. "For each work of art that becomes physical," said Sol Lewitt, "there are many variations that do not."

*

"Footnotes spring up like weeds in my mind as I write this" (Lillian Smith).

At the end of my long-ago first gig with Milton Dick and his Orchestra, I felt a strange combination of relief and overconfidence. It was no doubt the latter that led me to hop on the piano bench and strike up a tune I'd recently written.

Soon the pianist stood behind me. "What's that?" he said. I'd just fumbled toward a minor resolution.

"Something I'm working on," I said.

"You should write for the soaps, man," he told me and clapped me on the shoulder.

So much for overconfidence. I went right back to feeling like the inexperienced child (nightgown to my knees) I was.

*

In David Huddle's novella *Tenorman*, there's an "historical consultant" named Whitney Ballstom (a not-so-subtle evocation of jazz critic Whitney Balliet) who comments upon the titular tenorman's sudden blossoming: "There's even a new way he's using silence, letting half or three quarters of a phrase stand and then picking it up out of nowhere as if he'd been playing a whole sequence of notes in his mind without putting them through the horn."

*

I once wrote a short story called "The Rosebud Variations." In it—in what might have been a climactic scene—the narrator's invented fairy-tale heroine discovers what she believes to be a note left to her by her late mother, though it turns out to be an unfinished pencil drawing: *a self-portrait in which the left eye, the right half of the nose, the upper lip, and the very tip of her Woolfian chin had all been so often sketched and erased, then sketched again and erased, and again sketched and then erased again, that the face was nothing but a tornadic lead-gray blur littered with eraser dust—a face disappearing behind a mask of smoke.*

*

here in the darkness under the projector's beam a dust galaxy silently wheeling under the projector's beam in a chair he wakes silently wheeling on the screen his childhood in a chair he wakes like Odysseus on the screen his childhood to which he's been lashed like Odysseus forward out of the shadows to which he's been lashed issues his brother forward out of the shadows suntanned & bleach-blond issues his brother still clutching the air rifle suntanned & bleach-blond terrified of touch still clutching the air rifle run from your brother terrified of touch he watches himself turn & run from his brother in Technicolor he watches himself turn

& through bullet-gray woods in Technicolor imagines his silhouette through bullet-gray woods encircles him now imagines his silhouette nightfall incarnate encircles him now you won't hurt anybody nightfall incarnate rattling the chair he won't hurt anybody as the lashings snap rattling the chair & stands for a moment still as the lashings snap his brother dissolves & stands for a moment still soft-edged on the screen his brother dissolves in the center of his palm on the screen soft-edged a stone of absence in the center of his palm a dust galaxy a stone of absence he must carry smoldering in the darkness here

*

"[S]ome space in which mystery might still exist," said David St. John. Or as my partner, Kali, told me last Sunday on an afternoon drive (we were trying to get our kids to nap and have, for once, an uninterrupted conversation): "You are interested in voids."

*

A couple months ago, I had my creative writing students write a text to which no one could relate. *Is it even possible*, I wondered, *for a text to be void of relatable experience, emotions, or language?* As expected, we all failed—fascinatingly. My own attempt grew into "Nachträglichkeit (or, Landscape with Adventurers)," a poem in which a community awaits an unknown sound that they believe will signal a journey of transcendence into their town's surrounding ash trees.

Quite relatable—even to those for whom transcendence is a chimera, a fool's errand—because most of us have felt a desire either for the impossible or for what Ernst Bloch termed (in his introduction to *The Principle of Hope*) the *not-yet-conscious*, the *not-yet-become*.

*

I've long bristled at "relatability" as a rationale for an artwork's success. In the classroom, students will all too often describe a text as "relatable" because it's valid, true, and tends to foreclose further questioning from educators hesitant to pry into their personal lives. More importantly, however, I feel it rationalizes people's desire, consciously or un-, to remain safely within their own domains of experience; it rationalizes people's desire to read (and write) only "what they know" or what their sociocultural milieu tells them they should know.

*

"Cries of succor from its own unheard completion." Hidden in plain sight.

I hope readers of my work and of the work that matters to me (Wall's photographs, Hughes' *Ask Your Mama*, Shibasaki's *Spring Garden*, Carver's "Neighbors") can feel not only the provisionality of each compositional decision, but also the present absence of even prospective, untaken decisions—the not-yet-decisions. Ghost arms. Anticipation of the sensuous: words in the mouth or notes under fingertips. "Nothing that is not there and the nothing that is" (Wallace Stevens).

A new way he's using silence.
An invitation for you, too, to invent . . .

Bibliography

Adorno, Theodor W. "The Essay as Form." Trans. Bob Hullot-Kentor and Frederic Will. *New German Critique.* No. 32, Spring-Summer, 1984.

Alessandrelli, Jeff. *Biggie Smalls Skateboarding Superstar.* New England: Greying Ghost Press, 2017.

Ashbery, John. "The System." *Three Poems.* New York: Penguin, 1986.

Atwood, Margaret. *Power Politics: Poems.* Toronto: Anansi, 1996.
---. "Circe/Mud Poems." *Selected Poems: 1965-1976.* Boston: Houghton Mifflin, 1976.

Auden, W.H. "In Memory of W.B. Yeats." *The Collected Poems.* New York: Vintage, 1991.

Baldwin, James. *Giovanni's Room.* New York: Penguin, 1956.
---. "Everybody's Protest Novel." *Notes of a Native Son.* Boston: Beacon Press, 1983.
---. *If Beale Street Could Talk.* New York: A Laurel Book, 1974.
---. "Sonny's Blues." *Going to Meet the Man.* New York: Vintage, 1993.

Baudelaire, Charles. *Mirror of Art: Critical Studies.* "Exposition Universelle." Trans. Jonathan Mayne. New York: Double Day, 1956.

Baxter, Charles. "Against Epiphanies." *Burning Down the House: Essays on Fiction.* Minneapolis, Minnesota: Graywolf Press, 2008.

Bell, Marvin. "The Fifties." *The Jazz Poetry Anthology.* Editors Sascha Feinstein and Yusef Komunyakaa. Bloomington: Indiana University Press, 1991.

Bellamy, Edward. *Looking Backward: 2000-1887*. New York: Signet, 1960.

Benjamin, Walter. "Unpacking My Library: A Talk about Book Collecting." Trans. Harry Zohn. *The Art of the Personal Essay*. Ed. Phillip Lopate. New York: Random House, 1995.

Benson, Stephen. *Literary Music: Writing Music in Contemporary Fiction*. Hampshire, UK: Ashgate Publishing, 2006.

Berryman, John. *Stephen Crane: A Critical Biography*. New York: FSG, 1977.

Bidart, Frank. "Advice to the Players." *Music Like Dirt*. Louisville: Sarabande Books, 2002.

Bloch, Ernst. "Introduction." *The Principle of Hope*. Trans. Neville Plaice, Stephen Plaice, and Paul Knight. 3 vols. Cambridge: MIT Press, 1988.

Brown, Lee B. "'Feeling My Way': Jazz Improvisation and Its Vicissitudes—A Plea for Imperfection." *The Journal of Aesthetics and Art Criticism*. 58:2. Spring 2000.

Bök, Christian. *Eunoia*. Ontario: Coach House Books, 2009.

Borges, Jorge Luis. "August 25, 1983." *Sudden Fiction International*. Eds. Robert Shapard and James Thomas. New York: Norton, 1989.
---. "Blindness." *The Art of the Personal Essay,* ed. Phillip Lopate. New York: Anchor Books, 1995.

Calvino, Italo. "A King Listens." *Under the Jaguar Sun*. trans. William Weaver. New York: Harcourt, 1988.
---. "Introduction." *Italian Folktales*. Trans. Italo Calvino. New York: A Harvest/HBJ Book, 1992.

Carver, Raymond. "Neighbors." *Where I'm Calling From: Stories*. New York: Vintage, 1989.

Case, Kristen. *Abdication: Emily Dickinson's Failures of Self*. Essay Press. 2015.

Caspers, Nona. *The Little Book of Days*. New York: Spuyten Duyvil, 2009.

Chappell, Fred. "The Highest Wind That Ever Blew: Homage for Louis." *The Jazz Poetry Anthology*. Editors Sascha Feinstein and Yusef Komunyakaa. Bloomington: Indiana University Press, 1991.

Chopin, Kate. *The Awakening and Selected Stories*. New York: Penguin, 1986.

Christle, Heather. *The Crying Book*. New York: Catapult, 2019.

Ciardi, John. *How Does a Poem Mean?* New York: Houghton Mifflin, 1975.

Coleman, Wanda. "Jazz at Twelve." *Jazz and Twelve O'Clock Tales*. Boston: A Black Sparrow Book, 2008.

Connell, Evan S. *The Connoisseur*. Emeryville: Shoemaker and Hoard, 2005.
---. *Mrs. Bridge*. Washington, D.C.: Shoemaker & Hoard, 1959.

Conroy, Frank. "Think About It." *Dogs Bar, but the Caravan Rolls On: Observations from Then and Now*. New York: Houghton Mifflin, 2002.

Cortázar, Julio. "The Writer in a Trance: Anguish, Anxiety, and Miracles." *The New York Times*. 26 Jan. 1986.

Creeley, Robert. "Form." *Postmodern American Poetry: A Norton Anthology*. Ed. Paul Hoover. New York: Norton, 1994.

Crowley, Sharon. *Composition in the University: Historical and Polemical Essays*. Pittsburgh: University of Pittsburgh Press Digital Editions, 1998.

Delany, Samuel R. "About 5,750 Words." *The Jewel-Hinged Jaw: Notes on the Language of Science Fiction* Middletown, CT: Wesleyan University Press, 2009.

Derrida, Jacques. *Specters of Marx*. Trans. Peggy Kamuf. New York: Routledge, 2004.

Donaldson, Susan V. "A Stake in the Story." *Southern Cultures*. Volume 20, Number 1, Spring 2014.

Donish, Cassie. *On the Mezzanine*. Los Angeles: Gold Line Press, 2019.

Douglas, Ellen. *A Lifetime Burning*. New York: Random House, 1982.
---. "Advice to Young Writers." *Witnessing*. Jackson: University of Mississippi, 2004.
---. *Apostles of Light*. Jackson: Banner Books, 1994.
---. *Can't Quit You, Baby*. New York: Atheneum, 1988.

Dowling, Martin. "Thought-Tormented Music": Joyce and the Music of the Irish Revival." *James Joyce Quarterly*. Vol. 45, no 3/4.

Du Bois, W.E.B. *The Souls of Black Folk*. New York: Penguin, 1989.

Dyer, Geoff. *But Beautiful: A Book about Jazz*. New York: Picador, 1996.

Ellison, Ralph. *Invisible Man*. New York: Vintage, 1995.
---. "Living with Music." *Living with Music: Ralph Ellison's Jazz Writings*. New York: Modern Library, 2001.

Emerson, Ralph Waldo. "The Poet." The Collected Essays and Other Writings of Ralph Waldo Emerson. New York: Modern Library, 1950.

Espinoza, Joshua Jennifer. "Salt." *There Should Be Flowers*. Fairfax, VA: Civil Coping Mechanism, 2016.

Flaubert, Gustav. *Madame Bovary*. trans. Lydia Davis. New York: Viking, 2010.

Freud, Sigmund. "The Uncanny." <https://commapress.co.uk/>

Frost, Robert. "Two Tramps in Mud Time." *The Poetry of Robert Frost: The Collected Poems, Complete and Unabridged*. New York: Henry Holt, 1969.

Gilbert, Christopher. "Listening to Monk's *Mysterioso*, I Remember Braiding My Sister's Hair." *Turning into Dwelling*. Minneapolis: Graywolf Press, 2015.

Gilbert, Jack. "Less Being More." *Refusing Heaven*. New York: Knopf, 2009.

Ginzburg, Natalia. "He and I" and "The Little Virtues" *The Little Virtues*. Trans. Dick Davis. New York: Arcade Publishing, 1985.

Greenberg, Clement. "Towards a Newer Laocoön." <west.slcschools.org>

Halberstam, Jack. *The Queer Art of Failure*. Durham: Duke University Press, 2011.

Hardwick, Elizabeth. "Its Only Defense: Intelligence and Sparkle." *The New York Times*. 14 Sept 1986.

Hass, Robert. "Envy of Other People's Poems" and "Time and Materials." *Time and Materials: Poems 1997-2005*. New York: Ecco, 2007.

Hollinghurst, Alan. *The Spell*. New York: Viking, 1999.

Homer. *The Odyssey*, trans. Robert Fagles. New York: Penguin, 1996.

hooks, bell. *Teaching to Transgress: Education as the Practice of Freedom*. New York: Routledge, 1994.

Huddle, David. *Tenorman*. 1995. San Francisco: Chronicle Books, 1995.

Hughes, John. "Wordsworth's A SLUMBER DID MY SPIRIT SEAL." *The Explicator* (65:2). 2007.

Hughes, Langston. *Ask Your Mama: 12 Moods of Jazz*. New York: Art Farm West, 2009.
---. "The Blues I'm Playing." *Short Stories*. New York: Hill and Wang, 1996.

Ishiguro, Kazuo. "Crooner." *Nocturne: Five Stories of Music and Nightfall*. New York: Knopf, 2009.

Jackson, George. *Soledad Brothers: The Prison Letters of George Jackson*. New York: Coward-McCann, Inc., 1970.

Jackson, Reuben. "for duke ellington" and "sunday brunch." *fingering the keys*. Cabin John: Gut Punch Press, 1990.

Jacobsen, Karen. J. "Disrupting the Legacy of Silence: Ellen Douglas's *Can't Quit You, Baby*." *The Southern Literary Journal*. Volume 32, Number 2. Spring 2000.

James, Henry. "Preface." *Portrait of a Lady*. Hertfordshire: Wordsworth Editions, 1999.

Jones, Suzanne W. "Writing Southern Race Relations: Stories Ellen Douglas Was Brave Enough to Tell." *The Southern Quarterly* 47, no. 2 (2010).

Joyce, James. "The Dead." *Dubliners*. New York: The Modern Library, 1969.

Justice, Donald. "The Sunset Maker." *The Sunset Maker: Poems/Stories/A Memoir*. New York: Atheneum, 1987.

Kaufman, Bob. "Walking Parker Home." *Moment's Notice: Jazz in Poetry & Prose*. Minneapolis: Coffee House Press, 1993.

Kay, Jackie. *Trumpet*. New York: Vintage Books, 1998.

Koethe, John. "Introduction: Poetry and the Structure of Speculation." *Poetry at One Remove*. Ann Arbor: The University of Michigan Press, 2003.

Kunzru, Hari. *White Tears*. New York: Vintage Books, 2017.

Lanham. Richard A. *The Economics of Attention: Style and Substance in the Age of Imitation*. Chicago: University of Chicago Press, 2006.

Lawrence, D.H. "The Spirit of Place." *Studies in Classic American Literature*. New York: Penguin, 1977.

Levertov, Denise. "Some Notes on Organic Form." *Twentieth-Century American Poetics: Poets on the Art of Poetry*. Eds. Dana Gioia, David Mason, Meg Shoerke. New York: McGraw-Hill, 2004.

Levine, Philip. "A Dozen Dawn Songs, Plus One." <https://www.harpers.org>
---. "By the Waters of the Llobragat." <https://www.newyorker.com>
---. "Call It Music." <https://www.poetryfoundation.org>
---. "Gin" and "What Work Is." *What Works Is*. New York: Knopf, 2004.
---. "They Feed They Lion." *Selected Poems*. New York: Atheneum, 1984.

Lewitt, Sol. "Sentences on Conceptual Art." <http://www.altx.com>

Lopate, Phillip. "Notes Toward an Introduction." *Getting Personal: Selected Writings*. New York: Basic Books, 2003.

Lowell, Robert. "Watchmaker God." <babelmatrix.org>

Luter, Matthew. "The Multiply Framed Narratives of Douglas's *Can't Quit You, Baby*." *The Southern Literary Journal*. Volume XLVI. Fall 2013.

Madhubuti, Haki R. "Black man/ an unfinished history." "Gwendolyn Brooks." "Rise Vision Comin." *Liberation Narratives: New and Selected Poems 1966-2009*. Chicago: Third World Press, 2009.

Malamud, Bernard. *Dubin's Lives*. New York: FSG, 1979.
---. "Pictures of an Artist." *Pictures of Fidelman: An Exhibition*. New York: FSG, 1969.

Malech, Dora. "Love Poem." *Say So*. Cleveland: Cleveland State University Poetry Center, 2011.
---. "Q & A." *Stet*. Princeton: Princeton University Press, 2018.

Malouf, David. "An Die Musik." <poetrylibrary.edu.au>

March, William. "The Young Poet and the Worm." *99 Fables*. Tuscaloosa: The University of Alabama Press, 1988.

Matthews, William. "Masterful." *Search Party: Collected Poems*. Boston: Houghton Mifflin, 2004.
---. "Unrelenting Flood." *The Jazz Poetry Anthology*. Eds. Sascha Feinstein and Yusef Komunyakaa. Bloomington: Indiana University Press, 1991.

McCrae, Shane. "Horses Running Fast." *Mule*. Cleveland: Cleveland State University Poetry Center, 2011.

McKnight, Reginald. "This Is How You Get to the 40s." *Brilliant Corners*. Vol. 14, Issue 1. Winter 2009.

McPherson, James Alan. "Elbow Room" and "Why I Like Country Music." *Elbow Room*. New York: Fawcett Books, 1989.

Millhauser, Steven. *Martin Dressler: The Tale of an American Dreamer*. New York: Vintage, 1996.

Miranda, Deborah A. "Formula." *Indian Cartography*. New York: The Greenfield Review Press, 1999.

Montale, Eugene. "English Horn." Trans. Jonathon Galassi. *The Music Lover's Poetry Anthology*, ed. by Helen Handley Houghton and Maureen McCarthy Draper. New York: Persea Books, 2007.

Morrison, Toni. *Jazz*. New York: Vintage International, 2004.

Mullen, Harryette. *Sleeping with the Dictionary*. Berkeley: University of California Press, 2002.

Muñoz, José Esteban. *Cruising Utopia: The Then and There of Queer Futurity*. New York: NYU Press, 2009.

Norman, Brian. "James Baldwin's Confrontation with US Imperialism in *If Beale Street Could Talk*. *MELUS*. Vol. 32, No. 1. Spring 2007.

O'Connor, Jane. *Fancy Nancy's Fancy Words: From* Accessories *to* Zany. New York: HarperCollins, 2006.

O'Hara, Frank. "Ode to Michael Goldberg's Birth and Other Births." *Selected Poems.* New York: Knopf, 2008.

Ondaatje, Michael. "The Concessions." *The Cinnamon Peeler.* New York: Vintage, 1997.
---. *Elimination Dance.* London: Brick Books, 1999.

Ong, Walter J. *Orality and Literacy.* New York: Routledge, 2002.

Orr, David. *Beautiful & Pointless: A Guide to Modern Poetry.* New York: HarperCollins, 2011.

Parks, Suzan-Lori. "From Elements of Style." *The America Play: And Other Works.* New York: The Theatre Communications Group, 1995.

Pavlić, Ed. "*Stormy Weather* in a Time of Global Warming." <https://www.tiff.net>
---. *Who Can Afford to Improvise? James Baldwin and Black Music, the Lyric and the Listeners.* New York: Fordham University Press, 2016.
---. *Winners Have Yet to Be Announced: A Song for Donny Hathaway.* Athens: The University of Georgia Press, 2008.

Philip, M. NourbeSe. *Zong!* Middletown, Connecticut: Wesleyan University Press, 2008.

Poe, Edgar Allan. "The Red Masque of Death." *Edgar Allan Poe: Selected Prose, Poetry, and* Eureka. New York: Rinehart Editions, 1950.

Popa, Maya Catherine. "The Song of Male Aggression." *The Bees Have Been Cancelled.* Arizona: New Michigan Press, 2017.

Propp, Vladimir. *Morphology of the Folktale.* Trans. Laurence Scott. Austin: University of Texas Press, 1968.

Ratliff, Ben. "The Flying Modulation: Maria Schneider" and "I Know Who You Are: Ornette Coleman." *The Jazz Ear: Conversations Over Music.* New York: Times Books, 2008.

Rea, Robert. "Blues Tradition and Culture in Ellen Douglas's *Can't Quit You, Baby*." *Mississippi Quarterly.* July 2009.

Reed, Anthony. *Freedom Time: The Poetics and Politics of Black Experimental Writing.* Baltimore: John Hopkins University Press, 2014.

Reichel, A. Elizabeth. "Fictionalising music/musicalizing fiction: the integrative function of music in Richard Powers' *The Time of Our Singing.*" *SoundEffects: An Interdisciplinary Journal of Sound and Sound Experience*, vol. 4, no. 1, 2014.

Robertson, Lisa. *Nilling: Prose Essays on Noise, Pornography, the Codex, Meloncholy, Lucretius, Folds, Cities and Related Aporias.* Toronto: Book Thug, 2012.

Root-Bernstein, Robert and Michèle. *Sparks of Genius: The 13 Thinking Tools of the World's Most Creative People.* New York: Mariner Books, 2001.

Rosenberg, Harold. "The American Action Painters." *Art in Theory, 1900-2000: An Anthology of Changing Ideas.* Eds. Charles Harrison, Paul Wood. Oxford: Blackwell Publishing, 2003.

Ruefle, Mary. "I Remember, I Remember." <poetryfoundation.org>

St. John, David. "Memory as Melody." Where the Angels Come Toward Us: Selected Essays, Reviews and Interviews. New York: White Pine, 1995.
---."Note on 'Gin.'" *What Will Suffice: Contemporary American Poets on the Art of Poetry.* Eds. Christopher Buckley and Christopher Merrill. Salt Lake City: Gibss-Smith Publisher, 1995.

Self, Will. "Point of View: In defence of obscure words." *BBC.* 20 April 2012. <http://www.bbc.com>

Seth, Vikram. *An Equal Music*. New York: Vintage International, 1999.

Shelley, Percy Bysshe. "A Defence of Poetry." <bartleby.com>

Simic, Charles. "Crepuscule with Nellie." *The Book of Gods and Devils*. New York: Harcourt, 1990.
---. "Negative Capability and Its Children." *The Uncertain Certainty*. Ann Arbor: University of Michigan Press, 1985.
---. "The Singing Simics." *The Life of Images: Selected Prose*. New York: Ecco, 2015.

Sirc, Geoffrey. "Box Logic." *Writing New Media: Theory and Applications for Expanding the Teaching of Composition*, by Anne Wysocki, Johndan Johnson-Eiola, Cynthia Self, and Geoffrey Sirc. Logan: Utah State University Press, 2004.

Škvorecký, Josef. "Eine Kleine Jazzmusik." Trans. by Alice Denesová. *Hot and Cool: Jazz Short Stories*. Edited by Marcela Breton. New York: Plume, 1990.

Smith, Lillian. *Killers of the Dream*. New York: Norton, 1994.

Spencer, Sharon. *Space, Time, and Structure in the Modern Novel*. New York: NYU Press, 1971.

Spevack, Edmund. "Racial Conflict and Multiculturalism: Bernard Malamud's *The Tenants*." *MELUS*. Autumn 1997.

Spicer, Jack. "Song for Bird and Myself." *Moment's Notice: Jazz Poetry & Prose*. Ed. Art Lange and Nathaniel Mackey. Minneapolis: Coffee House Press, 1993.

Stafford, William. "A Way of Writing." *A FIELD Guide to Contemporary Poetry and Poetics*. Ed. Stuart Friebert, David Walker and David Young. Oberlin: Oberlin College Press, 1997.
---. "Improving Your Dreams." *You Must Revise Your Life*. Ann Arbor: University of Michigan Press, 1986.

Starnino, Carmine. "Lazy Bastardism: A Notebook." <https://www.poetryfoundation.org>

Stevens, Wallace. "Of Modern Poetry," "Peter Quince at the Clavier," "The Snow Man," and "Tea at the Palaz of Hoon." *The Collected Poems*. New York: Vintage, 1954.

Strand, Mark. "A Poet's Alphabet." *The Weather of Words: Poetic Invention*. New York: Knopf, 2000.

Tanizaki, Junichiro. *In Praise of Shadows*. Sedgwick: Leete's Island Books, 1977.

Tolstoy, Leo. *The Kreutzer Sonata*. Trans. David McDuff. New York: Penguin, 2004.

Tomash, Barbara. "Home Stead" *The Secret of White*. New York: Spuyten Duyvil, 2009.

tran, truong. *four letter words*. Berkeley: Apogee Press, 2008.

Twain, Mark. *Adventures of Huckleberry Finn*. Berkeley: University of California Press, 2001.

Villanueva, Victor. "*Memoria* Is a Friend of Ours: On the Discourse of Color." *College English*, Vol. 67, No. 1 (Sep. 2004).

Voight, Ellen Bryant. *The Art of Syntax*. Minneapolis: Graywolf Press, 2009.

Walton, Kendall. "Listening with Imagination: Is Music Representational?" *The Journal of Aesthetics and Art Criticism*. Vol. 52, No. 1. Winter 1994.

Wideman, John Edgar. *Hoop Roots: Playground Basketball, Love, and Race*. New York: Mariner Books, 2003.
---. "Williamsburg Bridge." *The Best American Short Stories 2016*. Edited by Junot Díaz. Boston: Mariner Books, 2016.

Williams, Patricia J. *The Alchemy of Race and Rights: Diary of a Law Professor*. Cambridge: Harvard University Press, 1991.

Woolf, Virginia. "Street Haunting: A London Adventure." *The Art of the Personal Essay*. Ed. Phillip Lopate. New York: Random House, 1995.

---. "The String Quartet." *The Haunted House and Other Short Stories*. New York: Harcourt, 1972.

Wordsworth, William. "A Slumber did my Spirit Seal." <poetryfoundation.org>

Wright, Charles. "Tomorrow." *Sestets*. New York: Farrar, Straus and Giroux, 2009.

Yeats, William Butler. "Adam's Curse." <poetryfoundation.org>

Young, Caroline. "This is not a No-Since; Multisensory Approaches to Teaching Gertrude Stein's *Tender Buttons*." *Teaching American Literature*. Vol. 8, Issue 3. Fall 2016.

Young, Dean. *The Art of Recklessness: Poetry as Assertive Force and Contradiction*. Minnesota: Graywolf Books, 2010.

Zabor, Rafi. *The Bear Comes Home*. New York: Norton, 1997.

Zucker, Rachel. *The Pedestrians*. Seattle: Wave Books, 2014.

Zurawski, Magdalena. *The Bruise*. Tuscaloosa: The University of Alabama Press (*FC2*), 2008.

Acknowledgments

Props to the editors of the following publications in whose pages portions of this book (often in slightly different form) first appeared: *Anastamos, At Length, Australian Book Review, Beloit Poetry Journal, Brilliant Corners: A Journal of Jazz & Literature, Columbia Poetry Review, The Collagist* (blog interview), *december, Entropy, Fairy-Tale Files* (blog interview), *Free State Review, Gigantic Sequins, The Hollins Critic, Hunger Mountain, NANO Fiction, Poet Lore, south: a scholarly journal, The Scores, Spillway Magazine, Spilt Infinitive, TYPO, West Branch, The Worcester Review,* and *Writing on the Edge (WOE)*.

"In Praise of Constraints: Inciting the Unexpected" was reprinted in *Far Villages: Welcome Essays for New and Beginner Poets*, edited by Abayomi Animashaun (Black Lawrence Press, 2020).

Portions of this book, in radically different form, also appeared in *A Love Supreme: fragments & ephemera,* winner of the 2019 *Quarterly West* Chapbook Contest. Several poems appeared in the chapbooks *as counterpoint to this compressed mass a longing* (Sutra Press) and *In Whose Hand the Light Expires* (Yellow Flag Press).

LAY OUT YOUR UNREST

www.ingramcontent.com/pod-product-compliance
Lightning Source LLC
LaVergne TN
LVHW051515070426
835507LV00023B/3129